Saltwater Cowboy

Saltwater Cowboy

THE RISE AND FALL OF A MARIJUANA EMPIRE

TIM McBRIDE

WITH RALPH BERRIER, JR.

ST. MARTIN'S PRESS NEW YORK

Certain names have been changed to protect the identity of some individuals.

 Printed in the United States of America. For information, address St. Martin's Press, 175 Fifth Avenue, New York, N.Y. 10010.

www.stmartins.com

All photographs courtesy of the author

Designed by Steven Seighman

The Library of Congress Cataloging-in-Publication Data is available upon request.

ISBN 978-1-250-05128-8 (hardcover)
ISBN 978-1-4668-8238-6 (e-book)

St. Martin's Press books may be purchased for educational, business, or promotional use. For information on bulk purchases, please contact the Macmillan Corporate and Premium Sales Department at 1-800-221-7945, extension 5442, or write to specialmarkets@macmillan.com.

First Edition: April 2015

10 9 8 7 6 5 4 3 2 1

To my son, Dalton, and my daughter, Kaila, this is who I am, and this is your legacy. You guys are and have been that which drives me every day, and you are the only two loves of my life.

To my father, Jack, who now watches over me from a silvery-lined cloud, I'm sorry I made you cry.

To my brother Pat, who I'm sure is standing next to Dad, telling him a joke, I now whisper into your ear, "I miss you, brother."

To my brother Mike, though we've been separated by vast distances our entire lives and though keeping in touch has never been either of our strong suits, please know that throughout the years I never lost sight of the fact that I have an amazing big brother, and he's always been just a phone call away.

To my mother, Dee, I'm sorry that if by my life's experiences I've caused your hair to turn prematurely gray. When I hopped into my Mustang and went south, my intentions were no different from those of any other young man. I left home to simply seek out a place in this world where I could stamp my mark. Thanks to you and Dad, I've lived my independent life by the seat of my pants and that philosophy of child rearing has set me on this path toward what I now know has been my first, best destiny.

To Tim Healy, for being the first to champion my story and for passing it on to Peter.

To Peter McGuigan and his family at Foundry Literary + Media, thank you for introducing my story to the world.

To my pals Ralph and Casey, thank you for guiding and governing my writing.

Saltwater Cowboy

PROLOGUE

The Gulf of Mexico smelled like cow shit.

Twice I drew in deep breaths because I didn't immediately recognize the odor. Cow shit? Out here on the open water?

I could see the cargo ship's silhouette as the giant orange sun sank toward the horizon. Then I heard them, bellowing, lowing. I couldn't believe it. The ship's stern gates were open, and the crew was using cattle prods to stampede an entire herd of cows into the Gulf of Mexico.

As our crab boat drew closer, the putrid smell of manure swamped us. Cows thrashed in the water, snorting, gasping, and groaning in panic as they climbed on top of one another, trying to keep their heads above water, their eyes rolled at the sky. Clark and I were too stunned to process what was happening. A herd of animals was drowning right in front of us. But as shocked as were, we knew we had a job to do. The cows were in the way.

As the ship's three-man crew looked down on us from the now empty deck, Clark and I tossed our lines at them to tie us off. I singled out the one who appeared to be in charge. He leaned against the rail, peeling an orange, so I hollered up at him, "What the fuck are you doing?"

He yelled back down to me matter-of-factly, with a Cajun accent, "I can't get the shit out of the hold with all these fucking cows in the way!"

The cows tried to herd together, *mooing* frantically with nowhere to go. They started sinking under, one after another. I freaked out a little until Captain Red put a calming hand on my shoulder.

"I told you that you wouldn't believe it," Red said solemnly as he turned away and walked the deck to the wheelhouse. The hard-bitten captain had known this stampede was coming, but that didn't mean he was cool with it.

The crew began throwing bales of marijuana down to us, ignoring the hopeless beasts. As the bales rained down, my buddy Clark and I stacked them forward, toward the wheelhouse. They were what we described as pillow bales, big plastic bags stuffed with merchandise inside burlap sacks, the ends stitched closed with twine. They weren't too heavy, but they were bulky, hard to carry, and took up a lot of space. Plus, some of the bales had already split and were spilling everywhere.

Behind us, another crab boat, our partner in this operation, plowed through a watery field of doomed cows. I watched as the animals banged their heads, horns, and hooves against the hull. As the crew pulled alongside us, no words were spoken. The looks on their faces said everything: *What the fuck was that?*

I looked at Clark. Loose shake covered his red hair and fair skin, turning his face bronze from resin dust. His cheeks looked like a pair of hamburger buns from all the pot seeds that had stuck to them. I started laughing. He took a look at my pot-covered visage and laughed for the same reason. We needed to laugh. This had been one strange night.

As the deck rapidly filled to capacity, we realized that we would need a different strategy if we were going to fit the ever-growing load onto our two boats and get it to shore. Captain Red maneuvered the boat so we could pile more bales onto the bow—and then on the roof of the wheelhouse around the radar array, and finally on top of the stern canopy that shaded us from the intense Florida sun.

The first stars of the Milky Way smoldered by the time we cast off from the cargo ship. The only parts of our boat that showed from beneath the mounds of bales were our front and side windows and the radar towers spinning overhead. We must have looked like a floating hay wagon.

I could not shake the image of drowning cows as we made the forty-mile run to shore. I looked back and caught a last glimpse of the cargo ship, which I imagined was heading south back to Colombia for another load of bales. And maybe another load of cattle, too.

I learned two things that night:

No. 1: Cows can't fucking swim.

No. 2: A million-and-a-half-dollar payday for a captain and crew was painfully and obviously worth more than a whole boatload of cattle.

It was our tradition: on the trip back, we took time to sample the goods. But on this trip none of us had brought a pack of rolling papers or a pipe, and not one of us had a match or a lighter to light the shit, even if we had. You would think a pot hauler would have these things. So we did the next best thing: we improvised by clearing off one of the deck hatches in the stern and placing a couple of handfuls of weed on top. Clearing the spot took a while because the shit was piled everywhere. But we then stripped the wire from one of our fish boxes and touched each end to the positive and negative posts of a twelve-volt battery that the captain kept in the wheelhouse. By doing this we produced a red-hot glow in the wire's center. Then, you simply touched glowing wire to the weed until it sparked. Clark blew on it like a Boy Scout making a campfire. When smoke began to billow, he held an empty five-gallon bucket upside down over the burning weed and let it fill up with the intoxicating cloud. When the bucket was full, we took turns placing it over one another's head. Our method was crude but very effective.

Having sampled the merchandise, we told the guys onshore how good it was. They kept a stash for themselves and put one aside for us. It wasn't a good idea to keep our own stash on board. We had to make sure that the boat was totally clean. When the off-load was complete, we steered a course back offshore to shovel the excess into piles and toss it overboard. Scrubbing the boat down from top to bottom was a meticulous and time-consuming task. Not a trace could be left anywhere on the boat.

After another job well done, the captain set a course for one of our trap lines and dropped anchor next to the end buoy. We really ran a crab boat after all. Part of the time, anyway. It was time to get some sleep. Later that morning, as the sun came up, we pulled that line of crab traps, then came in and unloaded our catch as if we had done two days of fishing.

I was right in assuming that our South American friends would come back with more. About two weeks later, we were off to haul again, and it turned out to be the same ship and crew. This time we were ready for the messy, loosely packed bales. Captain Red instructed us to line the entire deck with rolls of plastic and duct tape in order to make the cleanup process easier. After all, if we should happen to be boarded and searched later that night, a single seed could mean the difference between serving time and getting away unscathed.

Our two boats approached the ship the same way as before, except this time I noticed something different. This ship wasn't just carrying a herd of cattle. This time the SS *Ol' McDonald* had a variety of animals on board. Goats, pigs, a barking beagle in the wheelhouse window, and a dozen or so small monkeys scrambled over the deck. Later, I learned that monkeys liked getting fucked up on pot seeds and loose buds. They'd taken a nap among the bales when the ship was docked in South America and awakened as stowaways in the Gulf of Mexico.

When the stern gates opened in preparation for the off-load, those goddamn monkeys started freaking out and screaming, like they knew the stampede was coming. They took off climbing to the highest parts of the ship, all in a panic. They were on the bow and on top of the wheelhouse, and some were climbing the ship's radio antennas. Three of the little shits fought for the last space on the ship's light mast, alongside six others. I looked over at the wheelhouse just in time to see the beagle as it kept several of those critters at bay near an open window. Just behind that barking dog, the ship's captain kicked three monkeys out the door, screaming at them as he slammed it shut.

"God damn it . . . Get outta here you little motherfuckers!"

It was the funniest damn thing I'd seen in a while. Then, I saw the cows, doomed to their fate. Their asses would walk the plank.

After we got the load on board, Captain Red hollered up to the ship's crew.

"That's enough of this shit. You need to find a different way to do this or don't fuckin' come back!"

He climbed over the mountain of bales and made his way back to the wheelhouse. Inside, he rammed the throttle to full and the giant engine came to life with a muffled roar, belching plumes of black exhaust from the stern. As we pulled away, the thick cloud swept across the ship's now barren deck and draped all three of its crew in a fitting black shroud. Red was pissed, and we had his back. There was just too much work available and too many other willing captains and crews for us to be screwing around with clowns like those guys. These bastards just weren't seeing the big picture. Watching those cows drown was bad enough—what if they washed up on shore? I mean, it's one thing to be walking along the beach on a bright sunny day collecting seashells and you trip and fall over a dead fish. But it's a totally different thing to trip and fall over a fucking dead cow. It just ain't natural. Dead cows on the beaches of southwest Florida would be pretty suspicious in the eyes of the law.

When we got back to off-load the pot and I told the guys onshore that another load of cows just went to the Great Roundup at the bottom of the Gulf, they could hardly believe it. They had a good laugh at our expense, but I didn't care. I got paid $50,000 for each of those hauls.

From that night on, whenever our boat went out to bring back another load of marijuana, the guys had a name for us. We were the Saltwater Cowboys.

CHAPTER ONE

After a three-hour workout, I tossed a towel over my shoulder, picked up my water jug, and went for a walk to cool down.

Finding an empty bench was rare at that time of the evening, so when I saw one, I sat down for a while. I took off my shoes and socks, and I stretched my legs out so I could feel the cool grass under my bare feet. I sat there with each arm over the back of the bench and my head tilted back toward the evening sky.

Hearing the activities of others around me gave me a measure of contentment. There was the ricochet of a racquetball being struck, the ringing bang of a bouncing basketball, squeaking shoes as players ran up and down the court. I closed my eyes. I could hear an occasional jogger go past and birds singing as they prepared to roost for the night in one of the five trees in the yard. I opened my eyes in time to catch a glimpse of a moth drawn to the lights that had come on. It struggled against the same cool breeze that was drying the perspiration from my body.

This might sound like any of a thousand parks and any one of a million park benches in America. But this was the upper compound rec yard of the federal correctional institution in Tallahassee, Florida, and I was sharing it with 1,100 other convicted felons. It was 1991, I was the property of the US federal government, prisoner identification number 09498-018, and I was in hell.

I'd been here three years, and it was still hard for me to get used to the idea that I had seven more to do. It is a dose of harsh reality when you come to the realization that the world as you once knew it doesn't exist anymore. My whole world now was a little patch of land surrounded by two fences, separated by a twenty-foot stretch of land filled with razor wire, referred to as no-man's-land.

Every one hundred yards or so, those two fences met up with a concrete and brick structure that stood roughly fifty feet tall. Those were the half dozen or so gun towers. Behind the mirrored glass inside each tower were two armed guards standing vigil, their rifles in hand, just waiting to put a hole in your head should you decide to try your luck and make a break for home. If you were lucky enough to somehow make it past the interior fence, no-man's-land, and the exterior fence, you would surely be met by one of the two vehicles circling outside. Twenty-four hours a day, seven days a week, and three hundred and sixty-five days a year, those sentinels stood ready with their dogs and their rifles. The guards controlled the convicts' movements. That's what they called it—"controlled movement." They told us when to get up, when to eat, went to move from one area of the prison to another, when to piss, and when to sleep.

You see, there were only two ways for us convicts to get out of there. You either did your time like a good con, or you died. In a sense we were all castaways sharing the same desert island. Eating together, sleeping together, and growing older together.

That said, the most difficult obstacle wasn't the lack of control. It was the terrible feeling of loneliness and yet never being alone.

The time was nine thirty p.m., and over the intercom came those all-too-familiar words:

"Lockdown . . . Lockdown . . . All inmates return to your unit and prepare for ten o'clock count."

Everything began to wind down. All 1,100 of us would soon be locked into our units. I got out of my sweaty clothes and took a quick shower, then stood around bullshitting with a few guys near my cubicle.

Ten o'clock came and two guards approached. One remained at the door while the other shouted, "Stand next to your bunk, ladies, and shut up . . . It's count time!"

So we all stood up straight next to our bunks, and one by one we were counted, like cattle in a pen. The first guard to do the counting must have been a fucking moron or something because when he did his count, he would take a bean from one pocket and put it in the other for every con he counted. After completing his round, the second guard would repeat this process. Only difference was that this guy could remember his count. Afterward we were left standing there while he helped the dumbass figure out how many beans he had in his fucking pocket. When the count was done, the guards would leave and lock us in for the night. We would now have one hour to do whatever we cared to do until lights-out.

Every night at that exact same time, my buddy George and I played as many hands of gin rummy as we could until lights-out. George lived about eight cubicles away from me. I knew that he was locked up because he'd been a bank robber, and he knew that I was in for drug smuggling. But it was the kind of secondhand knowledge that was rarely, if ever, discussed. He was a man of many years—and by "many years," I don't mean just that he was in his mid- to late sixties. I mean that he had been there for twenty-eight years before I met him.

George was a kind man and very soft-spoken. When he did speak, it was with a slow Southern drawl. He stood only about five foot six, with a thin face and piercing green eyes. His brown hair was streaked with silver, and he liked to comb it straight back. He was like a father to me. Of course I had a real father, but that was in another life, in an alternate reality.

We could talk about anything, George and I, especially when one of us was having a bad day. Those days didn't often happen, but when they did, they were very emotional. You constantly trained your mind to leave your old life behind in order to live the new prison life that was ahead of you. But sometimes your mind just couldn't help but drift beyond those fences. You started thinking about how good it felt to be free. My friendship with George was a special one. We helped each other stay behind the fences. It was the kind of bond that is virtually impossible to achieve in the outside world—and often the only thing that allows you to keep your sanity in a world where insanity reigns. Playing cards was a ritual that helped get us through. We talked about what went on that day. Who got busted, who got his ass kicked. Any other prison bullshit.

But George must have been in a pensive mood that night because he asked me a question we'd avoided over the preceding years. It was the same question I had asked myself dozens of times after lockdown, as I lay on my bunk and stared at the ceiling. A question that, for no matter how long I considered it, I could never answer.

"Timmy, how in hell did you wind up here, anyway?"

CHAPTER TWO

How *did* I end up in prison? How did an outdoors-loving boy from the Midwest wind up as one of the most successful marijuana haulers in the United States? When you look back at my childhood and where I came from, you don't see the stereotypical story of a poor kid from a rough neighborhood who seems destined for a life as an outlaw. You see a kid who was born near a military base and who grew up in a nice neighborhood on a lake. You just never know how these stories are going to turn out.

I was born in Fayetteville, North Carolina. My father was with the 82nd Airborne, stationed at Fort Bragg, so I guess that makes me an army brat. My father's career went from jumping out of airplanes to jumping into them, as he traveled to every city on the East Coast, selling construction equipment. He was gone for months at a time, so I didn't see much of him while growing up. That was just how it was.

My mom went to work each day several towns over as a swimming instructor and an educator to children with special needs, jobs she held all through my early years. She taught my oldest brother,

Mike, to swim in the bathtub before he could walk. My middle brother, Pat, and I were taught to swim by age one. There was nothing out of the ordinary, nothing even the least bit dysfunctional in our family life.

My brothers and I were raised to be independent. However, if we strayed out of bounds by even the slightest margin and my old man was around to see it, he would snatch us back and make those boundaries very clear. Dad was a harsh disciplinarian. He grew up getting his ass whipped by his old man, and he believed it had made him the man he was. It was a tradition, traceable back to the days when young dirty-faced, barefoot boys would be sent on merciless quests to retrieve the very switches that would be used to emboss their fathers' message across their asses. It only made sense to my father to continue the tradition; he believed firmly in it. That was just the way it was in those days. Mom tried to follow suit in his absence, but we boys outgrew her gentler brand of discipline.

The memories of North Carolina are very vivid and very fun. My family's roots are in Ohio, so my grandma and grandpa, aunt and uncle (who was my mom's brother), and cousins shared a beach house with us each summer on Myrtle Beach, South Carolina. It wasn't all that far from where I was born, and the best part is that it was right next door to a miniature golf course. As kids we would play on the beach and in the surf during the day, and after dinner each night, right up until bedtime, we would play mini-golf. Then it was bedtime and the adults' turn to cut loose. They partied as we kids sat in the upstairs windows that overlooked the spinning windmill, the mysterious lost cave, the impossible maze. We could see the grown-ups as they drank, smoked cigarettes, and danced to the doo-wop and Motown that blasted from loudspeakers hung from lampposts, where strings of brightly colored lights lined the boardwalk.

As I approached my teen years, my father's sales career took off and he was given a Midwest territory that included Milwaukee and Chicago. I guess the company figured he could utilize either city's airport to keep up with his East Coast territories. So we settled in between, in Wisconsin, on the north shore of a lake that bears the town's name: Delavan. This is where I began and finished high school. And where I would be introduced to the leafy green plant that changed my life

This is how I remember my family's home. North Shore Drive is one of those lazy, shady, slow-winding back roads that, at times, tunnel their way beneath the branches of two-hundred-year-old oak trees. You can taste the cool, crisp lake air in the spring as it passes over your tongue like a sweet drink. The mailboxes and oak trees, those beautiful lake homes and brightly colored summer cottages, flit by like frames of a film. Just ahead a mailbox reads "McBRIDE." This is where you turn in. The driveway doesn't go all the way up to the house; it ends at the three-car garage just off the road. From there you take a quaint, but not very useful, flagstone path that winds through the backyard around a huge Sitka spruce and up to the house. When the home was built in the late 1800s, I'm guessing more thought went into its craftsmanship than how far it was from the road.

Once you enter, it immediately feels like home. No matter the time of year, there's a lingering hint of roasted firewood. Across the expanse of that spacious living room and just beyond the huge riverstone fireplace is the showcase of the home: a true picture window that spans the width of the house and affords a view so spectacular it looks like a painting. The lawn is greening up and attempting to show off its meticulously mowed and manicured surface—sculpted, of course, by yours truly. The flowers are soon to blossom in their beds, and the afternoon sunlight looks like fireworks on the rippling surface of the lake.

Look a little farther to the right of this scene and there are pieces of lumber of various sizes and lengths stacked neatly along the bank—that would be our dock. The lake is roughly a half mile across to the south shore here, at its widest, and stretches just a bit over four miles in length. A lake this size freezes over during winter, and the thick ice shifts and moves as the months pass. If the docks aren't removed from the water by October, they'll be locked in the frozen lake's grip; then the slowly shifting ice will have them splintered into firewood by December.

I remember this time clearly. It was the middle of May. I was sixteen, and my brother Pat was seventeen. Our big brother, Mike, was twenty and off to see the world as a proud US Marine. So this annual chore of reassembling the dock rested solely on our shoulders, and it was by no means a two-man job. So he and I piled into our hand-me-down powder-blue 1966 Chevy step-side pickup truck and took off for town to recruit a few friends to help us reassemble that pile of lumber in the front yard for the coming summer. It really wasn't hard, and it took very little time to get four of our buddies to sign on. Most of our friends came out and helped just to be there kicking back on the lake. We were back home with a crew in tow in less than an hour.

But before we began, the guys took a little walk out to the end of the driveway, past the mailbox and across the road. I followed, of course, curious to see what they were up to.

I knew about weed. I knew it was illegal, but I had never seen it and I had never smoked it. When one of the guys pulled out his pipe, I didn't give it much thought. Sure, I'd try it.

First came the flavor, then the stupefying shift in consciousness followed by a bout of coughing. Even at sixteen, I knew about the disastrous effects alcohol had on my thinking process and my overall ability to function, not to mention the wretched hangovers and disgusting expulsions of everything I'd had to eat or drink the day before. Smoking weed was so much different. I never lost control of my thoughts or my actions. Instead, I experienced hours of giddy excitement and random bursts of joyous laughter. It did not make me sick or hungover, nor did I have any regret for having smoked it. It was like the world around me had slowed its pace, allowing me for the first time to truly appreciate what it had to offer. The sights, the sounds, the smells that were suddenly awakened around me—they had always been there. What had been missing was a way to tune into this elusive sensory buffet. Mother Nature provided the means in the form of the contents of that little brass pipe.

The first time I tried marijuana, I found it difficult to keep a straight face as I reentered the house. The other guys and my brother went about their day as usual, and I . . . Well, let's just say I wasn't ready to build the dock quite yet. The boys made their way out the front door and along the walk to the steps leading down to the lake's edge.

At that moment my mom called out to me from what sounded like the other end of a long tunnel. I couldn't tell you what she was yelling about; I just knew I had to get out of there fast. But for each step I took toward the door, it retreated the same distance. Determined to escape, I made a lunge and caught it.

I went outside, where my brother and our buddies somehow

managed to put that dock together without any problems. We bullshitted and swam around for a while before returning to the house. There, every cabinet and pantry shelf in or near our kitchen came under siege. My mom was in the living room glued to the TV set, fully engrossed in a new episode of *M*A*S*H* and didn't even blink when six of us ran past her with the screaming munchies.

That summer turned out to be a blast, and getting stoned was the turning point. I saw that there was no harm done, no fouls committed. For the months that followed, my friends and I woke up early each morning to water-ski and trick-ski before the lake traffic made it too rough.

One of those friends was a guy named Clark. He was four years older than me, the same age as my oldest brother, and we became tight. He lived right next door, which made for easy access to the perfect ski boat, an eighteen-foot Chris-Craft Century inboard. As summer waned and school began, we skied before I went to class and again after. When the leaves turned, we donned our wetsuits and did the same, right up until the first snow.

When I graduated from high school, I had already been working as a machinist for a year through an on-the-job training program, and I continued to work for nearly a year after. Later, for about fourteen months, I had a full-time job in show business, more or less. I started working for Sammy Davis Jr. out in Los Angeles. My cousin Joey and his pal Hogan had this sweet gig driving Sammy's giant tour bus. When Sammy wasn't using it, Joey and Hogan chauffeured a fellow named Richard, Sammy's financial adviser, all over the country. I was getting tired of the same old routine, and when my cousin suggested I join him for a little hiatus on the West Coast, I split.

Turns out Richard and I hit it off great, and he offered me the job of videotaping Sammy's favorite TV programs for him. Besides being a financial wizard to a few stars, Richard owned one of the first video duplication companies in Hollywood. The era of the VHS cassette was just beginning, and Richard had a deal with most of the major motion picture houses of the day to duplicate movies from their original film versions to VHS tape on a massive scale. My duties included delivering these videos to his star clients and friends all over LA—Hollywood, Bel Air, Brentwood, Westwood, and anywhere else a celebrity lived. But my most important job was to visit Sammy once a week, wherever he was, and personally hand him a new *TV Guide* in exchange for one that he had marked up to show the programs he wanted to watch that coming week. All I had to do was sit in my apartment in Encino ("the Valley") and watch TV and movies. Most of the time, I just set them to record, took off down Ventura Boulevard and cut through Topanga Canyon to Topanga Beach, and threw a Frisbee with my friend Sean all day. Later, after an awesome day at the beach, I simply edited the commercials out of the programs, then walked Richard's dog.

It took about a year for my excitement over Hollywood to wear off, and I soon found myself driving back across the country to the lake, picking up right where I had left off.

While I was away, in the spring of 1978, my pal Clark had moved to Milwaukee, chasing a job. A year later, he called me to say that he and his girlfriend, Kat, were going to move to southwest Florida, where his sister ran a fish house with her husband. Clark had a plan. He was going to work on a crab boat, get high every day, and generally live like a beach bum. He asked if I wanted to go.

I had inherited from my dad a pretty wide independent streak, and I was eagerly looking for something better to come along . . . again. I had learned early in life that you should never pass up a promising opportunity. I dreaded the thought of looking back someday and kicking myself in the ass over something that I should have done. I'm not one of those guys who stands on his tiptoes in the back of a crowd, trying to see what's going on. I'm the guy elbowing and plowing his way to the front, because if there's some shit happening up there, I want in on it. So when my friend presented me with the opportunity—well, I did not hesitate.

"Hell yeah!" I said.

I just did it. I didn't even give two weeks' notice at work. I just threw everything I owned into the back of my Mustang Cobra with four bald tires and left Wisconsin the very next day. Just like that. My life was about to change in ways I never could have imagined.

CHAPTER THREE

I followed Clark and Kat in my Mustang Cobra, and we drove twenty-four hours straight to a pinprick on the map called Chokoloskee Island, a pile of sand, oyster shells, and trailer parks connected by a causeway from Everglades City, a speck of a town on Florida's southwest coast, with a neighboring population of just under five hundred souls. Chokoloskee Island turned out to be a 192-acre slice of heaven, tucked away in the northwest corner of Everglades National Park. People seemed to traverse the narrow streets by three primary modes of transportation: bicycle, golf cart, and bare feet.

I had no idea that day how well I would come to know and love this island and its quirky landmarks.

As we crossed the causeway, we passed the post office/laundromat. At the end of a dead-end street to the left, beyond the rows of trailers, was the only fish house on the island, Ernest Hamilton's Stone Crabs. Past that street was Ted Smallwood's trading post, which is now a museum. Most of the island's residents lived in trailers. There were occasional "houses," usually built up on stilts, most of which, I later learned, belonged to the families who were born and raised there on the island.

The island had a distinct and perpetual smell of low tide. Not only was it surrounded by water and mangrove swamp, but it seemed that every available open space was stacked with thousands of stone crab traps, which were waiting to be scraped of barnacles and other sea debris from the previous season, then dipped in a solution of diesel fuel and creosol. After the traps were drip-dried, new lines and buoys with a specific boat's identifying numbers branded on them would be attached.

Just past the Baptist church was Mr. Kelly's little general store, where a sign above the door welcomed you in with the words "Y'all Spoken Here." Before you put your hand on the old rusted screen door, Mr. Kelly would yell, "C'mon into the house!"

From the first moment I crossed the causeway, Chokoloskee Island felt like home to me.

Clark had lined up a job on a crab boat. He would be heading out into the Gulf of Mexico and bringing back loads of the island's chief delicacy. Me, I had squat. Soon, though, his brother-in-law hired me to work on his house, helping the carpenters and stonemason. I mixed the mortar and hauled blocks and stone for the fireplace up to the first level, and when I wasn't doing that, I was cutting and stacking lumber for the carpenters. It wasn't what I had come to Florida for, but I was a big, strong dude by this point, about six foot two, and 185 pounds of solid muscle, so I was equipped for physical labor. My physical features aside, if it involved a challenge, I was up for it.

In just those first few weeks on the island, I started to hear some local buzz about drug smugglers working the area, but it sounded like big talk to me. Until I saw it for myself, it was all just typical rumor crap.

I'd been down there about a month when Clark told me that there was an opening for a crewman on the crab boat he was working on. Second mate. I didn't know a second mate from a first cousin, but I told Clark that working on a boat sounded awesome. I wanted the job. I went down to the dock and met Captain Red, whom I expected to look like Captain Ahab, all sinister with a peg leg and a white beard and a long blue coat, tossing insubordinate crewmen overboard for shark food. Turned out that Captain Red was a measly five foot eight, as redheaded and as fair-skinned as Clark, and burned to a crisp. Frankly, he didn't look like the kind of guy who should spend too much time in the sun. His weathered face made him look older than he actually was. He had wavy hair and red stubble on his unshaven cheeks. He wore a flowery shirt, like any ordinary sandals-wearing, Bud-swilling beach bum Parrot Head you'd see at a Jimmy Buffett concert. Hell, he strolled on the dock with a baby under one arm and his wife hooked around the other. He was the coolest, most laid-back, family-friendliest Ahab I had ever seen.

He didn't say more than two sentences to me when Clark introduced us. But when Captain Red walked away grinning, I knew I had the job.

"Just play it cool, man," Clark said, rubbing zinc oxide on his bright-red nose. He popped Dramamine like Pez to ward off seasickness. (Even in our water-skiing days, he always was more of a landlubber.) "Captain Red just became a daddy for the first time. He needs a couple of good guys to keep the boat working. I vouched for you, man. You got the job. Let's go to work."

Stone crabs are a seafood delicacy found only in the waters off the southwest coast of Florida and the Florida Keys. I didn't know anything about crabbing, but I was strong and I figured I could handle sixty-pound traps filled with luscious stone crabs. I liked the physical work I had been doing in Florida, and I loved working outside in the sunshine. A job on the high seas sounded perfect to this Wisconsin boy. The next morning at three a.m., I reported to Captain Red's forty-nine-foot, twelve-cylinder, twin-turbo-charged Detroit Diesel–powered crab boat—disturbingly named the *Difficult Days*—and we set off before dawn from Chokoloskee Island.

The first thing I learned about the crabbing business is that there's not a lot to do until you actually get to the place where the crab traps have been set. I settled into my bunk to catch a couple more hours of shut-eye. When I rose with the sun, we were still chugging through the water. Clark set up a couple of fishing poles, and the two of us stripped down to cutoffs and kicked off our fishing boots as we motored deeper into the Gulf of Mexico. I tied a bandanna around my head and put on a pair of sunglasses and reclined on the engine cover. I felt like a hippie on top of a VW bus, except in the middle of the Gulf of Mexico. The only thing that would have made life better would have been if I could have fired up a joint—but I thought that might be bad form for the first day on the job.

Then Clark spared me the trouble: he fired up a doobie and passed it to me.

It'd be a while yet before we got far enough offshore to pull the traps that had been set the previous week, so I slipped back into my bunk in the wheelhouse, where Captain Red piloted the boat, and the steady rumble of the engine lulled me back to sleep.

About eleven a.m., somebody shook my ass awake. It was Captain Red, all five feet, eight inches of him, staring right in my face.

He was grinning as he casually drawled, "Timmy, we're not crabbing today, buddy. We're gonna unload a freighter full of pot. I'm sorry to tell you that now, but I wanted to wait until we got offshore."

He said it as calmly as if he was telling me he had to go to the john. What could I say?

"Cool."

That evening at sunset, rather than stone crabs, I was loading bales of marijuana onto the crab boat. Without any forethought, my life as a drug smuggler had begun.

I remember how exhilarated I was that day. Thrilled and excited, but also anxious. I had just made a decision, or had a decision made for me, to participate in an occupation that I thought was just a figment of the local imagination. Until that moment, I had believed in smugglers about as much as I believed in ghosts. Now, it turned out that the ghosts were real and I was going to be one of them, haunting the open seas. From that night forward, excitement and anxiety would battle it out in my mind every time I headed out on a job.

It was just the three of us on the boat that night—Captain Red, Clark, and me. Captain Red sat back in the wheelhouse and made radio contact with the pot-laden mother ship. The radio crackled with indecipherable Spanish and English conversations as Captain Red listened, cool as an ice chest, while plotting a course toward the scarlet setting sun. He was all business. He bantered with me and Clark—small talk, really. We could have been preparing to unload a cargo ship of cantaloupes for all the concern I heard. For his part, Clark was twitchy and ready to work.

We saw the lights of the South American ship we were due to meet. We were about sixty miles out from Chokoloskee Island now, out there in the Gulf of Mexico where people probably knew what those crab boats were really up to.

Things were moving fast for this Midwestern boy. The adrenaline was pumping. When we got to the ship, we loaded bales of pot like they were bales of hay. I figured the Coast Guard was watching our every move, but Captain Red stayed cool, watching his radar screen and listening to the scanners. We loaded the boat until I was sure it was going to sink in the middle of the Gulf; then we turned east and headed back to Chokoloskee Island. When we got to shore, all of sudden out of the darkness a fleet of small, fast boats—mullet skiffs and T-Crafts—sped to our boat like flies to a trashcan. Must have been twenty boats nosing in bow first. This job had to be done fast and furiously. Mates from the other boats jumped on board to grab bales from the mountain of weed. As soon as one boat's deck was stacked with pot, another pulled up behind it like a kid in a soup line holding up his empty bowl. Then, each one sped off to what I later learned were the stash houses, the places where the weed was stored.

The bales were all different sizes, wrapped in plastic and burlap. Flurries of loose marijuana snowed down on the crews and stuck to their sweaty skin as we tossed the weed onto their boats. Jesus, this was the hardest work I had ever done. We tossed pot all night, almost until sunrise. I had gotten only a few hours of intermittent sleep in the past twenty-four hours, and I had tossed a load of pot not once but twice—from the mother ship to our boat, then from our boat to the smaller crafts. When the last T-Craft had been loaded and our boat was empty, we headed back offshore. Captain Red ordered me and Clark to get down on our hands and knees to scrub the deck of every last sprig of marijuana. We scrubbed that deck cleaner than an operating room. I used a toothbrush and a screwdriver to clean between the deck and the rail and all around the hatches. Not a stem remained on board.

The next thing I learned about drug smuggling is that when the drugs are safely smuggled ashore, the crab boat has another task it must complete: actually bringing in some crabs. We idled near our line of traps, got some sleep, and awakened to a morning of pulling traps.

The next day, we did it all over again. Another load of pot, another night tossing bales onto speedy boats, followed by another day of crabbing. No rest for the weary, they say.

Two days later, I awoke to a pounding on the front door of the trailer I was living in. I shuffled to the door and saw Captain Red, all pink-faced and smiles—pot smuggler and proud father of a newborn—carrying a fairly large, fully stuffed paper bag.

We sat across from each other at the kitchen table. We made some small talk about where the redfish had been hitting around Indian Key Pass, and he thanked me for being such a good sport the other night. No problem, I muttered.

Red set the paper bag on the table and pushed it toward me. Open it, he said. I pulled out a bundle of bills, twenties. Then another bundle and another. I emptied $10,000 from that paper bag, my rookie cut for two nights of hauling thirty tons of marijuana. (Of course, I had no way of knowing that Captain Red had reaped about five hundred grand from the same two jobs. Rank does have its privileges.)

I had done good. He wanted me to keep working on his boat. He explained that he was just getting back into pot hauling and he hadn't trusted his last guy. He didn't know a thing about him, and in that line of work, trust was the most important job qualification in a prospective employee. Somebody had to know you and vouch for you. You didn't trust anyone unless you knew his family. But he trusted Clark and me. Clark's sister was married to a local, and that was good enough for Captain Red. Like they say, it's not what you know; it's who you know.

CHAPTER FOUR

Sure, smuggling was a lucrative occupation, but we were also a legitimate fishing operation by day. Clark and I were deckhands known as pullers—pulling the trap lines—but that job came with a price. Being a deckhand on a stone crab boat was the most ball-busting work I have ever done. But it was worth it because it allowed me to continue making the big cash by running offshore, climbing into the bowels of Colombian freighters or the holds of shrimp boats, and humping bales for more money in a week than the average Joe can make in three years.

In the months that followed, whenever Captain Red called me and said, "Timmy, we're going fishing," I knew he didn't mean that we were actually going fishing. Under his command, we smuggled at least three or four loads a month. After the first two trips, I wasn't a rookie anymore, so my pay went from $5,000 per night to $25,000 or even $75,000, depending on the size of the load.

As the sun set on the 1970s and rose on 1980, the work only increased for our small navy of crab boats and speedboats. One month we worked twenty-eight nights in a row off-loading pot from mother ships that were parked offshore, waiting for our arrival. At times, we had two and even three different fifteen- to thirty-ton jobs going on the same night. Through it all, we were just a bunch of ordinary young guys, playing pirates and making out like bandits.

The guys I worked with were cool, crazy dudes. Clark and I and the rest of us who worked on the boats offshore were taking the greatest risk because we were the only part of the operation to have sole possession of the *entire* load. This position put us at the top of the pay scale, and as a bonus we were the first to get our hands on each load. Clark didn't seem too well suited for outdoor work on the open seas, with his fair skin and susceptibility to seasickness. But he was strong, like me, and he loved physical labor. He and I spent almost every day together, either on a boat or partying in our mobile homes—which started to swell with brand-new televisions, stereos, speakers, furniture, and anything else we could blow our newfound wealth on. We bought new trucks and vans with cash—and we still had thousands of dollars stashed inside our homes.

One night, I rode to town with a friend in his piece-of-shit pickup truck with every intention of turning thirty grand into fifty hangovers and eleven bucks in change. When we got to town, I looked over at him and said, "Fuck this shit, pull in here."

We turned into a local car dealership owned by another friend of mine (my spending habits had earned me a lot of friends quickly on the Gulf Coast). I told my buddy to pick out a new truck. He made his choice, I paid for it in cash, and then we continued on our way. My friend at the dealership understood that he was to deposit the money in amounts under ten grand over a period of a few days—because amounts paid over ten grand needed to be reported to the IRS, and I couldn't have that happen.

"Now I feel better," I said as we headed out to party in his shiny new truck.

During those very early days of smuggling I met Danny, a crew member for one of the two other crab boats that had accompanied us on a particular off-load. He and his wife and young kids just happened to be my neighbors back on the island. Danny had an open nature. He held nothing back, and what you saw was what you got. He dressed in traditional island garb—only a pair of cutoff jeans, no shirt, no shoes. (Working on the Gulf waters and in and among the islands didn't require much of a wardrobe.) A few of Danny's uncles were the men setting up the smuggling jobs, I would later learn.

Danny and his two younger brothers were all involved in the "family business." He stood five foot ten and was, of course, fit and strong. His hair was mussed up like an ornery fifth grader's on picture day, including the little flip in front. Danny would probably be considered ADHD today. He was always moving a mile a minute, and if you spent the day and evening with him like we did, you were continuously sucked up into the whirling vortex of his energy field. There was literally never a dull moment with this guy around. He wouldn't let it happen—because he would fill it with something that was amazingly distracting. The dude could not stand still.

Danny liked to do a little trick he called "Skin a Cat," which involved shimmying from one boat to another across a nylon rope that tethered the two together. Sometimes he would try a trick where he'd slide headfirst down the top of a line and back up to the next boat. If he rolled over to the underside of the rope or fell off into the water, he failed.

The first time he proposed this stunt, nine other guys and I bet

$1,000 each that he could not make it from one boat to the other. Our boats were tied off to each other, bow to stern, and the length of rope between them was about fifteen feet. Without hesitation, Danny took hold of the rope and slid headfirst over the stern. All of us ran to the transom to watch him tumble into the water. Instead, he balanced himself so as not to flip over, then slid down the slick nylon rope, and then shimmied up the other side and climbed onto the bow of the other boat, $10,000 richer. It was the damnedest thing.

By then, we had become more established as smugglers, and our crews were known universally as the Saltwater Cowboys, our run-in with the cows on the high seas having reached legendary status. And I suppose "high seas" had a double meaning for us. We killed a lot of time on jobs sampling the goods that we were importing, all while cranking Lynyrd Skynyrd, the Allman Brothers, Led Zeppelin, and AC/DC. We were rock and roll kings. The bucking broncos of the Gulf of Mexico.

We filled our afternoons and nights with barroom stories of testosterone-fueled battles we had won or lost; then at last call we stumbled to the parking lot and hunted for our vehicles. One night, Danny staggered to his truck and doubled over to the pavement. He vanished for a moment, then popped up, his middle finger extended into the air. He wasn't flipping us the bird; he was twirling a pygmy rattlesnake like it was a lariat.

"Hey, look what I found!" he yelled. The damn snake had latched onto that finger and wasn't letting go.

When he realized that he had just been bitten by a fucking rattlesnake, he screamed to be taken to the hospital. On the drive there, he muttered, "Damn! It looked a whole lot easier when Marlin Perkins did it."

The motel bar and restaurant where we typically hung out on either a Friday or Saturday night was the Golden Lion. It was located just south of town, surrounded by glades and abandoned rock quarries that were created during the mining of materials used in the building of US 41 (aka the Tamiami Trail, a loose contraction of "Tampa to Miami"), the road that fronted the motel. The Golden Lion was one of only three options when it came to nightlife out here in bum-fuck nowhere. Then again, one could always generate one's own excitement in town. There was no lack of redneck imagination and ingenuity in Everglades City.

One time, this guy named Kalvin T. fucked up the pool at the Golden Lion by driving his airboat in it. We were all in the bar on a relatively subdued Saturday night when a few guests and their children came running through the bar with their Styrofoam noodles and blow-up floating toys, screaming about an asshole in the pool with his boat. A bunch of us left the bar and filed out back to the pool deck. As the glass door opened, a huge blast of wind and water soaked us and we were nearly deafened by the sound of an engine running wildly and belching unrestricted exhaust. Kalvin T. was drunk on his ass and in the pool with his airboat, turning 360s.

It reminded me of the first time I saw Kalvin T. I was on my way back to Everglades City from a grocery run to Naples with my windows down and the stereo up when I heard it. It was the unmistakable sound of a low-flying aircraft. I leaned forward over the steering wheel and cocked my head to the sky but saw nothing. As I sat back in my seat, I happened to glance to my left, and there in the tall saw grass next to the road was Kalvin T. and his airboat, keeping pace with me as he booked through the water. I looked down at my speedometer and the needle was splitting the 5 and the 0. He looked over at me, smiled, and put the hammer down on that

0-540 aircraft engine that was blowing him along and left me like I was tied to a pole. Just up ahead he eased over and, without slowing down, slid across the road right in front of me. Grass and debris and sparks flew everywhere. Then he was back off the road and into the tall grass, and just as quickly as he appeared, he disappeared.

We were crazy. We thought we were indestructible. That's a dangerous combination.

CHAPTER FIVE

I remember the first time I ever saw Darrel Daniels, part of a band of brothers who masterminded our little island organization. The Daniels boys—Darrel, Craig, Dwain, Randal, and Sherald—were the bosses, but everybody except Darrel always seemed to stay in the background, I would later learn. The boys and I were partying at a bonfire in the middle of the island woods one night, all of us pot haulers for different captains on different crab boats. A car radio provided a loud rock and roll soundtrack. Quietly, almost mystically, this dude stepped through the flickering shadows of the mangroves and strolled into camp. He looked old to me. Guy must have been at least thirty-five, I thought. He had a swept-up pompadour and looked like Elvis. His belly pressed hard against his shirt's abalone buttons, and it hung over, but could not hide, his gigantic silver belt buckle.

Everybody at the bonfire just stopped and stared. A few guys nodded toward the guy. "It's Darrel," somebody muttered. One of the good ol' boy godfathers. Darrel sipped at his Crown Royal and Coca-Cola and just hung out. He shot the breeze with a few of the boys, and then, just as mysteriously as he had arrived, he vanished back into the woods. I don't remember if I even spoke to him. But the captains often spoke among themselves and he knew who I was. They knew who stepped up to do the work, and they knew that I was a good worker. But if you had told me that night that I would be the guy who would succeed in perpetuating Darrel and his brothers' smuggling legacy, I would have told you that you were out of your fuckin' mind.

The day my fortune took the next leap began like any other workday.

By the fall of 1981, I had been hauling for about two years. Clark, Captain Red, and I had developed an unspoken language as we continued to work jobs together. On this autumn morning, the sun still sizzled. Clark smeared zinc oxide on his nose and took his Dramamine. As he climbed aboard, I gave him a sharp, direct punch to his triceps, a jab we called a "dead arm" because it made the victim's arm go numb. Boys will be boys, you know.

We were told that we were off to meet up with a ship offshore that would be carrying about sixty thousand pounds of Colombia's finest spring harvest. Three boats were arranged to haul the job, accompanied by a speedboat. Two hauling boats could manage it, but we decided to bring a third to carry that amount more comfortably and move it back to shore faster.

We had a nine-and-a-half-hour window to get the job done, from sundown to sunup. We had to intercept, load, and run the shipment to our smaller, faster T-Crafts and well boats waiting near the shore to take it to a stash house. A typical job for us.

We hooked up with the other boats at two o'clock that afternoon, with nearly five hours to kill before the ship reached us in the middle of the Gulf. The boat's radio blared over a loudspeaker. I stripped down to my jean cutoffs and jumped in the water and swam with the fish. Other guys dived into the refreshing water. We floated on our backs, swam beneath the boats from one side to the other, then climbed back on board to fire up a joint and cast our fishing lines in the water. Hard work.

At seven o'clock, it was finally time for Captain Red to make contact with the load boat: "Felipe, Felipe, Felipe, Zorro," he said over the radio. He chanted this call sign three times. We waited for a response.

Thirty seconds later it came: "Felipe, Felipe, Felipe, Zorro, come on."

And we were off to pick up sixty thousand pounds of weed. Or so we thought.

Just as the captains prepared to fire up the turbo twelve-cylinder Detroit Diesel engines in each crab boat, a small Cessna aircraft appeared out of nowhere.

It surprised the hell out of all of us as it dove like a kamikaze out of the sky, buzzing us from the stern and flying about twenty feet above the water. *Whoosh!* It flew so low it barely missed our radio antennas before it pulled up hard, then banked and rolled over to make another pass. That gave us all an adrenaline rush, but by this time most of us knew who this maniac was: Darrel.

Darrel Daniels, the mystery man from that night at the bonfire. But by now, I knew him and his five brothers well. The Daniels boys were fishermen who also happened to be hard-living, hard-drinking, hardworking family men. I'd learned that this ominous figure was nothing more than a good ol' boy. Like his brothers, he would go out of his way, day or night, to help a friend or anyone else, for that matter. Darrel loved to joke and fuck around as much as the next guy, to let his boyish nature out for a run from time to time—like now, flying above and buzzing us. He didn't actually have a pilot's license. He just had the cash to purchase the damn plane and the cash to hire a local pilot to show him how to fly it. Darrel was an easygoing guy who spoke with the distinctive Southern drawl of Jimmy Carter. He could lead a conversation the direction he wanted it to go without you noticing you were being led. That's a hallmark of a leader, and that's what Darrel was. He had a lighthearted confidence and was definitely in charge. And he was remarkably clever when it came to smuggling.

Darrel and his brothers Randal, Sherald, and Dwain had learned pot hauling from their brother Craig, who was introduced to it by the original smuggling legend, Loren G. "Totch" Brown. Totch was a first-generation islander, an alligator hunter and a tour guide who knew the rivers and swamps of the Everglades better than a New Yorker knows the subway system. When the fishing economy crashed in the 1970s, Totch discovered a new way to survive off what the Gulf provided. He started smuggling marijuana. Totch eventually served time in prison, and he renounced his pot-smuggling legacy in his later years before he died in 1996, having become something of a Gulf Coast celebrity.

Anyway, when his smuggling days ended, the Daniels boys were ready to take it up a notch.

We looked up at the sky to see what the hell Darrel was up to in that plane. As he made his next pass, Darrel threw a plastic milk jug out of the cockpit window. It tumbled through the air and splashed into the water, and when we hauled it in, we pulled a note out from inside the jug: "One of your boats needs to break off and head to . . ." followed by a series of numerical coordinates. "There's another vessel waiting there to be unloaded. Go!"

Radio contact in this line of work was not a very good idea. Radio frequencies could easily be scanned by the Coast Guard or marine patrol or whoever else might be out there listening. This was Darrel's solution: an airdrop and a message in a bottle.

Bringing the third big boat along was a good idea then, as it turned out. Our boat stayed with the original job, and one of the other two peeled out after a coin toss. The chase boat stayed with us. That's the lightning-fast speedboat, which was there for us to jump on and make a hasty escape if the Coast Guard caught up with us. Mike was the chase boat captain, and he was the very best. Our boat had paid for the protection of Mike's Scarab, and there was no way in hell we were letting him go. So the guys on the boat that left us would just have to toss their load overboard and make a run for it if they had a problem tonight.

We headed for our original destination, twenty miles west of our current position, accompanied by Captain Mike's Scarab and by Captain Black Ass and his crew.

Captain Black Ass was awarded this nickname by the men who worked for him, and who had endured the hard-core work ethic he hammered down. The name was an odd choice for a five-foot-six, 145-pound white guy, but his dark demeanor and smart-ass attitude made "Black Ass" the perfect irreverent handle. When crabbing, he dressed in overalls and a T-shirt and walked the deck in white fishing boots, snarling commands. But when he was pot hauling, he turned into a jovial, happy-go-lucky guy. Still, with only one look, he could convey to his crew, *You can fuck around today, but tomorrow your ass is mine again.*

We approached the load boat earlier than usual that evening because we had to haul more than usual. As our target came into view, we saw that this was obviously not a boat in the traditional sense of the word. It was a *ship*. A freighter, to be exact; at least three hundred feet from bow to stern.

Clark and I looked at each other at the same time.

Holy shit.

Even then I realized: What we were staring at was the result of that thin blue line that separates supply and demand. A whole industry springs up to work around it. And everyone—from shipping companies to bankers to airport managers to customs inspectors to cops to local politicians—was in on the act. All of them made more money than all the honest cops in Florida combined. As I looked at the giant freighter rolling on the sea before us, I realized that our little business had now become, officially, an *industry*.

We were still about a mile from the ship, and we could smell the familiar odor of pot and burlap in the air. Mike slammed his throttles to run ahead of us, throwing a wide rooster tail twenty feet in the air as he circled in front of the ship. He did this to fire up the crew and to get everyone's blood pumping, and in his own way to tell the crew of the freighter that it was time to start getting that shit up on deck: *Here we come.*

The giant ship's weather deck was twenty feet above the waterline. That meant the bales had to be dropped sixteen feet down to our deck. Now, these bales weighed seventy to a hundred pounds *each*. Tightly packed and sealed in plastic secured with duct tape with a final covering of burlap, they were compressed and packaged this way to ship the maximum quantity possible. A far cry from the pillow bales we were used to and had complained so much about. We hated cleaning up after hauling pillow bales, which shed marijuana like the Scarecrow from *The Wizard of Oz* lost his straw. After some face-to-face meetings with the captains, the bales had become more compact.

But the new bales were not exactly what we'd had in mind. Sure, we no longer had to shovel piles of weed from the deck, but now these fuckers were going to be a *bitch* to handle.

With thirty thousand pounds to take aboard each of our boats, we would have to stack over four hundred pieces per vessel. There was also the fact that these heavy-ass blocks were going to be *dropped* on us from sixteen feet up.

Because the deck and rail of the freighter were so high above us, we couldn't tie our boats off. In order to keep them against the side, Captain Red and Captain Black Ass had to keep us positioned tight against that giant ship—otherwise the shit would drop into the water. It's no easy task lifting a seventy-plus-pound bale of pot with no handle out of the water and onto the deck, especially when the next one is falling right after the last.

Now, there must have been at least sixty men on that ship that I could see, and probably a couple dozen more below. These guys marched in single file through a hatch leading down to the hold and came back up through a different hatch with bales on their shoulders. Each man took his turn throwing a bale overboard to our deck below, and it was only after the first dozen or so hit the deck that we started to hear cracking sounds. The deck was beginning to give way.

Although our boats were built with reinforced fiberglass, there was no way they could take the beating of these fucking bombs hitting, one after another. And it was increasingly difficult to keep up with the pace these sixty-plus guys were setting. Our inability to keep up actually saved our boat, it turned out. As the bales piled up, they cushioned the blows of the next ones and prevented the decks from being smashed to pieces.

We filled our front hold, then our midship hold, and started stacking bales on the deck and bow. Just like with the "cattle jobs," we put the shit everywhere we could think of as the bales continued to fall.

Because our boats were designed to haul crab traps, by their very nature they were perfectly designed for hauling pot bales, which were within twenty pounds and a handful of inches of being the same size and weight. The open deck was thirty-eight feet in length with a twelve-foot beam (the width of the deck from rail to rail). So there was plenty of room for this load, or so we assumed.

But as we stacked bale after bale, with the deck almost three-quarters loaded, we knew that we should have already taken the entire shipment by now. I yelled up to the freighter captain standing by the rail: "How much more?"

In broken English, he yelled back, "Feeftee more."

But after fifty or so more bales we yelled again, "How many more are there?"

Cupping his hands around his mouth, he shouted, "Feeftee more."

By this time the scupper holes of both our boats had begun to dip underwater. The scuppers are openings around the upper deck that allow water to drain from the deck back into the sea. But as our boat got heavier, the scuppers nearly had the reverse effect of letting water pour into our boat. Immediately, we began plugging the scuppers with foam that we cut from one of our life jackets so we wouldn't start taking on water and sinking.

Meanwhile, Captain Dumb Shit up above kept raining down bales on our boats. Fifty more, my ass. Either this jackass couldn't count or he was out of his mind. We loaded more bales until we absolutely could not take another. One more bale each and both boats would have ended up on the bottom of the Gulf of Mexico.

We said the hell with this shit and pulled away, fast. Our boats were more overloaded than they had ever been.

It was very slow going back to the shore, and we shook our heads as we left those guys, who were tossing the extra bales overboard off that gigantic ship, cheering us on, yelling, "*Rápido, amigos, rápido!*"

They continued to toss bales overboard until we lost them over the horizon behind us. There must have been 80,000 pounds or more on that freighter and at least 15,000 to 20,000 pounds of it went right into the Gulf that night.

As time went on, I learned that this sort of miscommunication happened quite often. It prompted us to coin the term "square grouper." That became code over the radio for those bales that never made it aboard our boat or fell off during the voyage back to shore. We would relay the message to one of the shore crew back on the "hill," referring to where we docked and kept our traps, and the news would spread like wildfire that there were square grouper offshore. The next morning whoever wanted to could go and collect.

It would get this way from time to time each year. When the work got more and more frequent, usually during the fall harvest, which was the largest down in South America, the owners of the merchandise shipped more than we expected, thinking that we'd just take it on. It was because of bullshit stunts like those that we haulers started insisting that one of their men accompany the load from the origin, typically northeast of the city of Barranquilla on the Guajira Peninsula on the Colombian coast, back to Miami. This soldier would be involved every step of the way and be held responsible for the counting of each and every piece, along with one of our men, who was paid specifically for the same purpose. That way if anything happened to the shit, regardless of whether the suppliers had to throw it overboard or abandon their vessel, their guy would be right there with it when they did, leaving no unanswered questions.

Now, these guys on this huge vessel had been traveling with this shit for more than eight days, and if there was no other vessel there to take the balance, they had no choice but to toss it and get the fuck gone.

It wasn't the first time I'd seen it. In those early days of pot hauling, there was just too much of the shit coming in for one crew to handle. Every now and then we would get word that this crew or that crew had been chased by the law and had to throw their load overboard and vanish into the night. More often than not, the circumstances were justified. But occasionally a crew just got spooked and tossed the shit off the boat, sparking a free-for-all.

One morning around four a.m., on our way down the shoreline to pull traps, we plowed through a school of square grouper. Clark and I were sound asleep in our bunks when we were suddenly awakened by our acting captain kicking the bunk.

"There's bales out there, boys!"

We jumped up, put our boots on, and flew out of the wheelhouse. As we stood on deck at the rail, a full moon lit up the predawn sky and shined down on the water, revealing the silhouette of bales as far as the eye could see. Herb, who was Captain Red's dad and our temporary captain, was busy calling Red on the radio to come and retrieve our bounty. Overhearing that call was our go sign to get busy pulling it out of the water and stacking it on the deck. By the time we stumbled upon this floating treasure, the seawater had already begun to saturate some of the bales. There were so many, though, that we could take our time and pick out the ones that were still floating high in the water. It was our intention to pass them off to Red's smaller, faster boat and continue on with our day of fishing, tongue in cheek.

Not wanting to risk overloading the boat—but well aware the bales were valued at more than $20,000 each—we rescued forty pieces. We figured that was enough. It didn't take long for Red to arrive, and with our share of the free pot safely on its way to a hiding spot among the islands, we continued on our way to pull a line of traps.

Around midmorning a few friends in a frantic search passed by our boat while we were working and asked us where the bales were floating. Herb told them where they could find the stuff, even though by this time the current would have had them drifting hard and spread out for miles. He also informed them that by now the bales might be tough to see as all of them were probably soaked and floating at water level. That fact wasn't going to stop the searchers. We had all been through this before. The stuff could still be dried and sold after the salt water was rinsed out of it. That's exactly what we would do with the sections of ours that were wet, and since ninety percent of what we had plucked from the sea was dry, there was very little that needed to be rinsed out anyway.

After we finished our day of pulling and returned to shore, Herb and Clark took a ride to the hardware store in Everglades City to purchase a large roll of nylon screen and a few rolls of duct tape. I stayed behind to fill a fifty-gallon drum with freshwater and load it onto a smaller backwater boat.

After dark we took that boat into the mangrove forest among the islands where our stash was hidden, and we separated the wet stuff from the dry. The dry stuff was left in its plastic-and-burlap wrapper and resealed with duct tape, then loaded onto the boat. The remaining wet stuff—about four hundred pounds' worth—was rinsed with freshwater taken from the fifty-gallon drum. We spread the weed out to dry on sections of screen that we strung like hammocks between the trees.

On the way back home that night, with nearly two thousand pounds of dry pot, I learned that we already had a buyer waiting for us. The roughly four hundred pounds that was still hanging in the forest needed time to dry, then would have to be sampled before a price could be negotiated. None of us expected to get top dollar for that part of it because the salt water and rinse tend to reduce potency. Still, this was all found money to us, so we were going to maximize the stuff's earning potential.

Clark and I took charge of the drying process. Over the next two nights we returned to flip the weed so it would dry evenly and not mildew. On the third night we were ready to bring it home. But Clark and I failed to time our departure with the tide, which was already falling when we arrived. While we were packaging the now dry pot in plastic bags, the tide had completely gone out and left our boat high and dry, resting in the mud. By our calculation the water wouldn't return for at least another six hours. We were screwed. We spent a miserable six hours battling giant mosquitoes and dry throats. Nothing could be done about our thirst, but we did have a solution to our mosquito problem. It was a simple matter of burying ourselves in the mud and covering our mouths and eyes with our T-shirts, then waiting.

After what seemed like forever, the moon did its job, bringing the water back in and floating our boat. Clark and I got the hell out of there. At around three a.m. that morning, the two of us were met at the dock by Red, his dad, Herb, and the buyer. The next evening, after another day of fishing, the four of us split the $940,000 of free money that we'd found literally floating on the water.

Anyway, back to the night that the big freighter overloaded our boats. Now our problem was getting this oversized load to shore. We had less than eight hours to travel thirty miles, meet the smaller boats, and off-load the cargo—all before the sun came up. We were totally exhausted, but we were on our way, and we thought the long cruise would allow for a well-needed rest.

But it was on our way back that we noticed a severe vibration in our propulsion, followed by a noise like a cannon shot: *BANG!* The enormous strain on the wheel from the weight of the load had caused one of the propeller blades to break off.

You could not freak out at a time like this. Captain Red hailed our sister boat, which, fortunately, was right beside us. Radio communication at this stage of the operation—or at any part of it, really—was out of the question. Clark and I immediately climbed out of the wheelhouse, over the stack of pot, and onto the bow. We untied our anchor rope from its leader chain and began uncoiling and doubling it up, braiding the two halves together to make one thick rope. At the same time, Captain Black Ass and his boys were doing the same to their anchor rope in preparation to tow us in.

Captain Black Ass positioned his boat in front of ours as we rigged our boats for towing. His crew took hold of one end of our rope as we took hold of the other end of theirs. They tied off their ends to each side of their stern.

The strain on the ropes was going to be tremendous, so in order to tie their ends off securely, they had to run the towlines through the scuppers by pushing one through the port side and one through the starboard. That way we could use the entire stern of their boat as a bridle. Normally, this wouldn't have been an issue except that the scuppers were plugged, stuffed with foam to keep the boat from sinking. If the foam was removed to open the scuppers for the towline, the boat would take on water.

Once again, this was no time to freak out. Black Ass's men pulled out the scupper plugs one at a time and then reached over the stern into the water and pushed the ropes through, repacking the foam around them and tying the two ends together, while all of us were seconds from going under.

With their end of the towline secured, we secured ours to the Samson post on the bow, a ten-inch-by-ten-inch solid piece of wood that extended from above the bow down to the keel, where it was bolted and fiberglassed into place. The ropes stretched and strained under the terrific force, but they held. And we were moving again, though *very* slowly.

Between the thrust our boat could supply with a broken prop and the pulling power of our towboat, we were traveling at about half the speed we should have been. Normally, we liked some chop and a bit of rough weather or even a storm. These events helped lessen the threat of coastal patrols being out here. But that night, if the seas had not been calm and the skies had not been clear, we would have been fish bait. We prayed for calm water.

After we got the train rolling again, Captain Mike suddenly appeared beside us in his Scarab. I sat back on the huge stack of pot on the bow and breathed a big sigh of relief, rolling a fat joint. I looked up at the stars and thanked my lucky ones and whatever gods were up there as I raised it to Mike, cruising alongside us now. He acknowledged me by raising his own fatty. Man, it felt great knowing that he was there.

When you're at sea, far away from the glare of city lights, a billion stars shine above. Except for them, the darkness stretched out in every direction of the compass. With the moon having left us hours before, this blackness became our cloak now. Only the trail of the excited phosphorous churned up by our wake betrayed our presence. The trail faded behind us as quickly as it appeared.

After all that, we made it back in time to off-load before sunrise.

And because some bonehead in either Miami or South America had seriously screwed up in estimating the load, I made $80,000 that night, double what I had expected.

That's just the beginning of this story.

CHAPTER SIX

The next day the bales began their journey to Miami. This was when the good citizens of Chokoloskee Island did their part. I had just awakened after having been offshore all night, and the shore crew was in full swing. I took a stroll across the island to the stash house, and as I rounded the corner, a car engine fired up. One of Danny's two younger brothers closed the trunk with his wrist so his fingerprints wouldn't make the journey as well. He gave a quick kick to the rear bumper with his fishing boot, and the driver took off. To those of us living on the island who were aware of what was going on, it seemed that the place was buzzing with the activity of pot smugglers and our helpers. From the point of view of those who did not have a clue what we were doing, it seemed like just another hustling-and-bustling day on Chokoloskee.

With a load this size most everyone on the island got involved with the haul—even the women. Guys in cutoffs and T-shirts and gals in bikinis and halter tops mobilized like it was a denim-clad Normandy invasion. The bales were moved from the stash houses and were loaded into cars with the backseats removed, hollowed-out vans, and pickup trucks with camper tops. The suspensions were rigged with inflatable airbags, which lifted the vehicles up to compensate for the added weight of the load. Then, after the vehicles were emptied, the drivers simply let some of the air out of the bags and the ride returned to normal for the trip home. This time, we even loaded a Winnebago, which had been stripped of everything below the window line with a chainsaw and wrecking bars. The cabinets, curtains, and everything above the window line were left in place so that if someone looked through a window from outside, everything appeared normal. The RV was loaded from the back to the front and stacked right up to the bottom of the windows with a little over nine thousand pounds of weed. All the seats had been removed, and a makeshift driver's seat was fashioned among the bales in order to take advantage of all available space. I had to give the guys and gals of Chokoloskee Island a lot of credit. It took guts to drive this barge all the way to Miami. That was one part of the operation that I always told myself I wanted no part of—ever. It was far safer out on the open water with a chase boat at my side.

The load was ready the next morning at daybreak to be shipped overland to the east coast of Florida, 120 miles across the southern tip, down US 41 through the Everglades. All of these smaller loads were going to a plaza in Kendall, a suburb on the west side of Miami, where our drivers would pull in and park, then get out and go do a little window-shopping. Because the vehicles were sent in staggered intervals, usually at about twenty minutes, one member of our crew, a "spotter," would be paid to simply stay there all day and point out those vehicles to our Miami partners waiting to receive them as they arrived. Their men got in them and drove them the rest of the way to a stash house, unloaded the bales, then returned the vehicles to our drivers. Our drivers headed back to the Everglades in their empty vehicles—even picking up and delivering another load, time permitting.

These "dead drops" (a term coined by the government to describe our method) were a safety precaution designed to make sure that our drivers had no idea where the stuff was actually located in Miami. On the other side of the coin, the guys in Miami could have no idea where the stuff was coming from in the Everglades. Trust was ensured by mutual uncertainty.

But a single shipment this huge couldn't be delivered to the same place as our typical, smaller loads. There was too much risk and too much money at stake. It needed to go directly to the stash house in Miami for off-loading.

You could say I was in the wrong place at the wrong time, and then again you could say I was in the right place at the right time. I tend to believe it was the former and not the latter. Either way, Darrel turned to me and asked:

"Timmy, would you be willing to drive this one to Miami for me and then stick around for the rest of the day? There are several large bags of cash I need brought back to me tonight."

I had dreaded this moment. I'd just come by to lend a hand emptying the house when Darrel realized that he didn't yet have a driver for this behemoth.

"I need someone with brass balls, and it has to be someone I can trust," he said.

"Thanks, but—"

"If you do this for me, there's another thirty-five thousand dollars in it for you."

That added up to $115,000 for one night of work. That was a big incentive. But in truth, it wasn't for the money that I agreed to do it. It was the fact that Darrel was saying he trusted me to bring back his three-quarters of a million dollars. I was scared at the idea of it, but I was also honored. It took King Kong–size nuts to do shit like this, and my face was becoming familiar in places where crazy shit like this was happening on a regular basis. I had been involved with every stage of the game up until now.

Darrel handed me the keys along with a two-meter radio so I could keep in touch with the road crew.

"Good luck."

I got into the houseboat on wheels, crawled across the sea of bales to my makeshift driver's seat, cranked the ignition, and took off down the road.

I must admit that in all my years of hauling pot I was never so fucking freaked out as I was that day behind the wheel of that $4 million rolling block of weed. The two hours it took to make the trip felt like a hundred years.

But once I got onto the highway, my fears diminished. I became fully focused on the task at hand. And there was a small level of comfort in knowing that there were other guys on the road, too. They were ahead of me and behind me, watching out for highway patrol or any other signs of law enforcement. Nobody ever traveled alone.

But it was definitely a *small* level of comfort. If for some unlucky reason I should happen to get tagged by a cop, I was sure as hell not going to outrun them in this motor hotel. I had two options: One, I could just give up and say fuck it, you got me. Two, I could grab my radio, climb over the bales to get to the door, jump out, and haul ass.

As I lumbered down the road in the laden Winnebago, I decided that if it came to it, I would choose the latter. I'd take my chances in the swamp rather than just give up, I told myself.

But that option wasn't very good either. There were a lot of obstacles to safety with that choice. They included, but were not limited to, alligators, crocodiles, water moccasins, rattlesnakes, pygmy rattlesnakes, black bears, panthers, bobcats, wild boar, black widow spiders, fire ants, and, of course, swarms of mosquitoes so thick that I would not be able to breathe.

If I managed to survive the Wild Kingdom of Death, I would still have my radio so I could contact my buddies and tell them where to come and find my ass.

If I had been driving one of the smaller cars, there might have been a third option. The guys and gals driving cars, vans, and pickup trucks were all equipped with raised trailer hitches. If they were stopped, they could simply back up into the cop's car and puncture its radiator, which would set off the air bag in the police car. With the cops disabled, they could haul ass down the road until they met up with a spotter. Then they could jump out, leaving the bales and the vehicle on the side of the road as a prize for the cops while they disappeared. Then it was a simple matter of reporting the vehicle stolen.

But that strategy was off-limits to me in this traveling museum of felonies.

I cranked up Pink Floyd as I put it all out of my mind and cruised into Miami.

Run, Rabbit, run . . .
Dig that hole, get the sun.

Two hours later, I'd made it.

I arrived at the turn to the stash house, and the road meandered through an old orange orchard that had obviously been neglected for a few seasons. The house finally appeared, and it seemed strangely out of place. Where you might have expected to see a split-level, Southern-style estate home and Spanish moss draped over live oaks, you found a behemoth—a fifteenth-century medieval-castle-looking thing. A couple of Cuban dudes were there waving me up to the side of the house next to a double set of cellar doors. I put that big bitch into park and climbed over the bales and jumped out. As their crew began the unloading process, the guys who were in charge invited me in for a cold drink, something to eat, and a friendly game of poker. One of the dudes, whom they kept referring to as Flaco, which in Spanish means "skinny man," led the way through a side door that took us straight into a huge kitchen. Adjacent to the kitchen was a large dining table that easily seated twenty. It reminded me of the one Errol Flynn leaped across with sword drawn to rescue the lovely Maid Marian from the would-be ravages of that prick sheriff. And just beyond the table was the lounge area where I spent the rest of my stay, relaxing on plush tucked-and-rolled leather sofas, sipping on sweet tea. (I didn't touch the hard stuff on a job. Too much money was at stake for me to get hammered.)

The rest of the deliveries continued coming in, and as we sat there, I noticed the way these guys were treating me. It was almost as if I were a celebrity.

It got me thinking: These guys didn't have the balls to do what we did on a daily basis. That would explain why we were the ones moving all this shit for them and the fact that we were moving it virtually unmolested.

I was flattered by their curiosity. A guy asked me what it felt like to take that kind of a risk out on the highway, risking my life, driving a Winnebago full of weed.

"It feels like I just won a one-hundred-and-fifteen-thousand-dollar jackpot," I said.

Later that evening, they gave me a car to drive back to Everglades City with five bags of cash in the backseat.

If I thought driving a Winnebago full of marijuana to Miami was terrifying, driving back with three-quarters of a million dollars in cash right behind me had me shitting my pants the whole way home. But I made it, and Darrel was grateful to the tune of thirty-five grand.

From that day forward, if I wasn't on the boat offshore unloading freighters, I was in Miami being the "spotter," pointing out our vehicles as they entered our dead drop location for our Cuban partners, whom I soon got to know pretty well. And they got to know me, too.

To them, and everyone else involved on their end, I was a man who was trusted—by both sides. I appreciated our new relationship. I also had no idea just how quickly these new friendships would be a boon to my career.

But for now there was just the money. More of it than a twenty-five-year-old knew what to do with. I bought gold and diamond jewelry, new cars, new boats, new trucks—even houses—and I still didn't know what to do with all of it. Sometimes I would take an exotic vacation to a destination picked out by simply blindfolding myself and pointing at a map of the world. I would often bring friends with me and pay their way just to have someone along for the ride. Pissing away sixty grand or more at a time was a common occurrence. Many times several of us would take twenty grand each into town and buy drinks and cocaine for everyone in the bar until most of the money was gone. Then at closing time, we'd tip the bartenders and waitresses a couple hundred bucks each to unload the rest. Go home, pass out, and get up and do it again. It just kept coming and coming and coming.

CHAPTER SEVEN

"Lights-out."

The disembodied voice boomed from the front of our prison unit. I tossed my cards down on the bunk.

"I'll tell you more about it another time," I said to George. "Good night, my friend."

The lights went out as I made my way back to my bunk.

Well, one more day down and only several thousand to go, I thought.

The next morning, I awoke to another day as an inmate and got myself ready for work. My original assignment was working construction within the prison, but I quickly decided, to hell with this horseshit. If I have to work, I may as well work smart and not hard.

One of the first guys I met when I got here was Rolando, Rolly for short. Rolly was already into his fourth year and had another twelve to go on a counterfeiting charge. He was half American Indian, half Puerto Rican, and was born and raised in the Bronx. He was in his early thirties and was already balding and sported a dark mustache. At first glance, you'd swear he was Wally Cox, a TV actor who used to play nerdy roles and who was a regular guest on

The Hollywood Squares in the 1970s. Rolly had himself transferred to the library in order to further his education. He and I became friends and workout partners.

We were spotting lifts for each other on the weight pile one day when he said to me, "There's an opening for another con in the law library where I work. Do you want the job?"

"Damn right I do," I told him. "Get me in!"

That afternoon he took me down to the lower compound into the education building and introduced me to the head con in the law library. His name was Dennis, an older guy probably in his mid-fifties. He was a perfect Captain Kangaroo look-alike. At first glance, I could see that the years had really taken their toll on this guy. Twenty-two years of prison life had chiseled away at his face, and it would be another thirty years before the sculpting was complete.

Dennis had been given fifty-two years for bank robbery. At the time, this ridiculously long sentence was listed in *The Guinness Book of World Records* as being the most time given for this particular offense. He was the pilot of a small Cessna aircraft that was used to fly away the two guys who pulled off the robbery. Even though he didn't actually rob the bank, he was charged for it as if he had been there and given a huge sentence. As for the other two fellows who had actually robbed the bank, one was sentenced to nine years and the other got twelve years. According to Dennis, the reason he had gotten so much time was because, for many years prior to the bank job, he had been flying rather large quantities of cocaine from Mexico to Nevada. All the years he was doing this, he had been under suspicion but never caught. When the federal authorities finally had something to charge him with, they decided to make up for all the lost time spent trying to catch him with cocaine. So they hammered him with fifty-two years for this one bank robbery.

Anyway, he took a long, hard look at me. He asked me my name and how much time I had to do. I told him my name was Tim and that I had a "dime," which meant ten years, and I wasn't interested in doing my time building this goddamn prison. He laughed.

"Hell, you've got the job, Timmy."

He liked me right away.

The next day, paperwork was sent through assigning me to work with Dennis and Rolly. It was a pretty easy gig. I spent my days studying law and helping other cons do research for their own cases. It was, for the most part, an out-of-the-way place. A con could work alongside civilian teachers and other vocational instructors (male and female) from the outside. More important, he could be left alone. For the entire educational center, two guards were assigned, roaming the halls to keep an eye on the cons who were taking classes.

The educational center was a safe place. It was totally night and day from anywhere else in this prison. Like the rec yard, for instance. There, it took very little provocation to get your ass kicked by any number of different cliques.

I came to realize that the library job was a rather prestigious spot within the prison hierarchy. If you were the only guy who a con could turn to for help with his case, guys were less likely to try to kick your ass over stupid shit. Because if you messed with me, you were also messing with about a hundred other cons—guys whose cases would not be taken care of now because of your bullshit. Not only that, most of the cons had already paid for my services. Yeah, that's right, they were paying for my expertise. I wasn't about to give this lawyer shit away for free. Everyone in the joint had some kind of hustle going on to try to make an extra buck. You were either working in the kitchen selling sandwiches, hard-boiled eggs, or anything else you could get your hands on or you were doing other cons' laundry for them. And there were those who wouldn't hesitate to be the "punk in your bunk" for a new pair of tennis shoes under theirs. This was just the way it was and still is. There really wasn't any way to survive in prison making a lousy six cents an hour working a prison job, and that even was after a couple of raises. If your family or your friends were not putting money in your account, then you had to rely on yourself and learn to hustle. We were allowed to have a maximum of fifteen dollars in change on us at any one time, so I would just tell the cons who owed me money to have someone on the outside deposit it into my account. Then I used that money at the commissary to buy things that helped make my life just a bit more comfortable. I could buy things like a new pair of tennis shoes or new socks, new shorts and shirts, or a couple of dozen packs of cigarettes to pay for stuff on the prison black market. I could even treat myself and a few of my pals to a pint of ice cream when the commissary was open once a week.

The job came with other perks, such as being able to change my schedule as I saw fit. For instance, in the winter I worked during the evening hours. That allowed me time to pump iron on the weight pile during the day while it was sunny and a bit warmer. During the summer I worked through the hot days, taking advantage of the education building's air-conditioning, and pumped iron at night when it was cooler. I soon realized that by working in the education building I had inadvertently surrounded myself and made friends with a better class of convicts. I know that's not saying much, but this was the world in which I lived. One more friend made was one less con willing to step up and try to kick my ass or take my life when the shit in prison went sideways.

I studied law and worked on other cons' cases for three years and was pretty good at it. Another summer came and went, and I returned to the evening shift. After several hours in the library, quitting time arrived and I left the building. The cons who didn't work in the education building were counted out first by the guards. After they left the building and the count was cleared, the cons who worked in the building were counted out. The guards knew exactly how many came in and how many went out so there was no doubt that everyone had left the building.

At nine thirty p.m., over the intercom came those all-too-familiar words:

"Lockdown . . . Lockdown . . . All inmates return to your unit and prepare for ten o'clock count."

During those long dark nights, George got out the cards and started talking and asking questions again about my life on the outside. One subject he never brought up, though, was women. He didn't have to.

Women? Damn right there were women! But there's always that one who manages to get under your skin and stick around. In my case, there was only one who was remotely worthy of discussion. No amount of concrete or steel bars could separate me from that vision of her.

CHAPTER EIGHT

I met Lori in the summer of 1982 at the Even Odds nightclub in Naples where she tended bar. She was twenty-two years old with meticulously curled blond shoulder-length hair. Her smooth, tanned skin gave a vague scent of coconut. Her eyes were as green as Colombia emeralds. She had the body of an Olympic athlete and looked like a character from a Jackie Collins novel, whose bikini lacked enough material to cover that which the designer had intended. Five feet, eight inches of pure hot-ass woman.

When we first met, Clark and his girlfriend, Kat, had become homebodies who never wanted to leave the island. Even though he was my best friend, I had to get away every once in a while and cut loose with the boys. My buddy Todd and I led a group of about a dozen "weekend warriors," fellow smugglers who made the thirty-mile drive to Naples to party. I didn't even drink in those days. But I sure as hell liked to dance.

I didn't care much for the post-disco club music, though. I loved classic rock and roll. Led Zeppelin. The Rolling Stones. Florida boys Lynyrd Skynyrd, obviously. While Todd and our crew bought rounds of drinks for two hundred of their closest friends, I tore it up on the dance floor. Our favorite club had five separate bars on three different levels, but our little group of single guys usually gravitated to Lori's bar because, well, she was the hottest and most outspoken little shit tending any of them. She took good care of the boys and me, and we took good care of her. As the nights unfolded, so did the twenty-dollar bills. We threw our cash around like it was Monopoly money. We stuffed her tip jar with fives, then tens. By last call the guys were fucking around—throwing wadded bills at one another, stuffing each of the wine and cocktail glasses hanging above the bar with twenties. This went on every night we came to town.

"Are y'all bank robbers?" Lori asked one night.

"Nah," I said, playing it cool. "Just pot haulers."

"Bullshit." She threatened to call the cops on me.

Lori was a Gulf Coast yahoo, with a mouth like a Chokoloskee crabber. Before long, she was my girl.

Lori was as passionately erotic and energetic as she was beautiful. She could step right from the shower, skip the makeup, and still look like she had spent an hour in front of the mirror. Her Friday night ritual was to enjoy an ice-cold Michelob Light while she got ready for our night out. She said the beer buzz got her in the mood to dance. So I cranked up the tunes and rocked the house while she did her thing. She dressed in the latest fashions. In those days, the girls either wanted to look like Debbie Harry from Blondie or, a couple of years later, like Madonna, but Lori pushed the limits of fashion. I can still see the looks on people's faces in the summer of 1983 as Lori strolled down South Beach wearing her new thong bikini. This was truly a first, even for South Beach. Talk about turning heads. She wanted to be the woman everybody looked at when we walked through the doors of a nightclub. She came in screaming, hootin' and hollerin', carrying a drink somebody had put in her hand before she hit the dance floor.

As for me, I really had no sense of style. I felt more at home in the mangrove swamp and Everglades bush. Cutoff blue jeans, a T-shirt, and no shoes were my typical island garb. Lori, however, wanted to be my wardrobe assistant, and she dragged me kicking and screaming into the 1980s. Before long, she had me dressed the way she wanted: A nice, buttoned-down shirt with the sleeves turned up and shirttail loosely tucked into a pair of black parachute pants. A skinny tie never pulled up tight to the neck. High-top Reeboks, untied. Hair trimmed tight and the face sporting a five o'clock shadow. The ensemble was not complete without gold necklaces, diamonds, gold rings. I really looked the part of a pirate.

Lori continued to work as a bartender. We both worked; it had to be that way.

That's how it came to be that she knew everybody and everybody knew her. When we settled on a club for the night, we'd claim our spot, usually the champagne room, and have the run of the place. She danced and mingled with anyone and everyone. She was like a top that keeps on turning until its momentum gives out, which in her case was at about three a.m.

Everywhere we went, every bar, every nightclub, people knew that Lori was with me. If some poor sap came on to her, she would simply laugh in her own cute way and tell the guy, "Don't even think about it!" Then she nodded in my direction. I wasn't the jealous type, I never have been. Yet when a guy got stupid with Lori, watch the fuck out. She was a firecracker; she could handle herself. And a simple nod from me to any one of twenty or so other guys would have that fool's question answered for him before he could ask it, anyway.

Lori was ambitious, to say the least. While working, she danced from one end of the bar to the other in her Daisy Dukes and bikini top. She was a master in the business of mixology and gratuities, which she skillfully blended into your very own personalized erotic cocktail. She mixed one part straightforward business sense with a splash of cutesy finger-on-cheek suggestiveness and had all the boys drinking out of her hand and stuffing her tip jar. After a time, she took a break from bartending and opened a floral shop at the locally famous tourist destination Tin City, a gathering of waterfront shops and restaurants in old downtown Naples along the Gordon River. Her sister was her partner, her mother was their support system/gofer, and I was the financier. Floral Fantasy was the name on the wall out front, and inside it teemed with beautiful floral arrangements, bouquets, ferns, and a numerous variety of trees all made of silk. The business was tailor-made for the bustling tourist industry, which is why we chose to open in Tin City. When Lori took a sudden interest in dipping her toes into business, I was eager to take a dip myself, although I had an ulterior motive. I needed a way to justify my recent purchase of an $80,000 chase boat. Floral Fantasy provided the perfect cover for where the money was really coming from. I named the boat *Pair A Dice*, and she was a beautiful black-and-red-over-white thirty-foot Chris-Craft Scorpion powered by twin 200-horsepower Offshore Mercury outboard engines mounted on Gil brackets, which extended her length to thirty-five feet. I spared no expense, of course, and she was loaded with extras: wraparound seating in the stern covered in thick tucked-and-rolled cushions, which sported the same black-and-red-on-white scheme; the gunwales and deck were covered in a brilliant white nonskid gel coat; and the center console, where the captain kept his toys, separated the stern from the midship compartment, where there were three equally comfortable seats. Sitting in the captain's seat was a geek's wet dream. All the gauges and switches for the bilges, blowers, and electrical systems on the control panel were lit up, including the hand-held radar, LORAN-C navigation system, colored sonar bottom and depth finder, VHF radio, and Polaris scanner. In the bow section was a portable head and a small galley and table next to a pile of soft pillows on a king-sized soft bed.

I had made a deal with one of the local scuba dive shops, who agreed to take me through the various levels of certification to bring me to Divemaster status. In exchange I allowed him to hire/charter my vessel as his exclusive transportation to the open waters of the Gulf, where he could properly certify his students at every level. The course was intense and the training was rigorous and exhausting, but once that little card with my picture and Divemaster rating on it was put into my hand, the final piece to my plan was in place.

I displayed a beautifully enlarged picture of my new dive boat in the girls' shop along with all of the information necessary for people who wanted to charter her. So what exactly was the plan? It was simple, really. In the state of Florida, a fishing or diving charter business is considered a service and is not required to pay the state a sales tax. Hence no reporting, and hence I would sit down at my kitchen table and literally write imaginary charters into the books for the purposes of laundering a few dead presidents. The money I made from chartering the boat was negligible compared to the overall scope of my business of smuggling, but between the chartering and the occasional trip to the Bahamas, the charter business generated a fairly decent amount of spendable cash. It was also important for the boat to be seen and to become a familiar fixture coming and going up and down the Gordon River and in and out of Gordon Pass during the day and night. Lori and I used it often and, as always, we had an entourage. If we spent the day on the south end of Keewaydin Island, a long thin barrier island spanning the coast between Naples and Marco Island, the supplies would include everything needed to barbecue, stay stoned, drink, and dance around a beach fire until the wee hours of the morning. Lori didn't smoke weed. She was more interested in what was in the cooler. If we headed offshore for the day to swim and scuba dive, all the gear necessary for six divers to go into the water at one time was on board, and most of the supplies were the same.

A lot of the people we hung around with weren't divers, so I would give quick lessons in the pool before leaving the house. They got accustomed to breathing under water in a relaxed environment before jumping off of my boat into the open ocean. My brother Pat was one of my quicker studies, and as it happened, his first diving experience was a night dive in about thirty feet around a shrimp boat that had sunk while trying to tow a barge.

I was introduced to scuba diving out of necessity rather than sport. On a crab boat, you are bound to wrap a few trap lines around the wheel and shaft. Sometimes the tide will pull the lines in the wrong direction and the boat will run them over, or you miss the buoy that marks where the traps were laid and it vanishes in the propeller wash when the captain throws the boat into reverse. Either way, when the accumulation of line becomes too great, the spinning shaft ties itself into a solid ball of nylon with a fuzzy coating. The tangle of lines pulls the shaft and its giant four-hundred-pound brass wheel out of balance, and the entire vessel begins to shake itself apart. Even if the boat can limp back to shore, nobody is going home until someone goes overboard and cuts that shit free. One thing was certain, the captain sure as fuck wasn't going over the side. So Clark and I would take turns each time the dirty deed needed to be done. The lucky guy stripped down to his briefs and, with a knife in hand, dove in and swam under the boat and wedged himself between the strut and the hull. The rudder rests in a "shoe" on the end of the strut, which allows it to swivel hard over port to starboard, also known as "lock to lock." And the shaft and wheel are centered in front of the rudder between the two. With your back firmly against the hull and your feet planted squarely on the strut, you would saw on that big black ball as long as you could hold your breath. When you surfaced for air and to exchange your now dull knife for a freshly sharpened one, your mate was right there waiting for you. This part of the job was done regardless of the weather, the sea conditions, or the temperature, and depending on how much line was down there, you could be in the water for some time. This part of the job was dangerous, and it sucked.

One of us finally came up with the idea of scuba gear as a possible solution to making repeated dives, reducing the dangers of swimming beneath a pitching and rolling boat. Clark and I went to a Naples dive shop, where we purchased two masks, two buoyancy compensators, and two tanks. You needed open-water diver certification in order to get oxygen tanks refilled, but we didn't have it. What we did have, though, was lots of cash, and with that and a wink we always got our tanks refilled. After a few lessons from an instructor in exchange for letting him charter my boat, I was a scuba diver.

Lori was not the least interested in diving. She was a swimmer, a water skier, and a sun worshiper. She remained on deck of the *Pair A Dice* with the other girls in the party while the guys and I explored the wreckage on the sea bottom. Our typical days of sun and scuba usually ended with a thirty-minute, fifty-five-miles-per-hour cruise to the dock, where we ditched our friends and took another fifteen-minute drive to the house, a ten-second sprint to the pool, followed by a two-second free fall into bliss. A nice cool plunge into a freshwater pool after a long sunny and salty day felt like taking off a suit made of cracker and washing out hair made of three-day-old cotton candy. Lori and I had two hours to kill before she began her shift at the bars and I took off back offshore—again. That was our routine.

Between my disappearing for days and her perpetual party life as a bartender, we didn't really have much time to work on our relationship. That began to take its toll. I can't count how many times other bartenders, twenty or more friends, and the occasional club owner would follow us home after hours of partying. Lori and I rarely had any time alone together. When I wasn't around, the parties happened somewhere else, and eventually she stopped making it home at all. Mass quantities of liquor will ultimately strip away your inhibitions like a flaming curtain from a window, and all your secret demons are right there with their faces pressed against the glass.

By the summer of 1986, we'd been together about four years and my life had become less about the money and more about the moments. In Lori's world life had become more about the money and less about the moments. For all the good times spent on loving and laughing, there were equal numbers of bad times spent on damage control and cleanup. That good stuff attracted us and kept pulling us together like two magnets. As nice as that was, I have to say that if you introduced me to the most beautiful woman on this planet, I'm pretty sure I could introduce you to the guy she drove nuts.

CHAPTER NINE

In the early 1980s, the US government stepped up its efforts to shut us Saltwater Cowboys down. Our little hole in the Everglades was an embarrassment to the Feds, so they initiated two operations designed to stop the flow of Colombian and Jamaican marijuana and cocaine into southwest Florida. In the first of these attempts, Operation Everglades in 1983, more than two hundred agents descended upon our Gulf Coast backwater like the Gestapo in hopes of taking down the whole deal. They raided homes. They seized property and boats. They blocked the causeway. They tore through the narrow streets. They caught twenty-eight guys, which was surprisingly few, considering that the entire damn island was in on it.

Operation Everglades was a total federally sponsored clusterfuck. It was as if Barney Fife were running a bunch of Keystone Cops. Police couldn't even get to the houses for all the reporters who had converged on our streets. It was the first traffic jam in the history of all 192 acres of Chokoloskee Island. "There's about one reporter for every one that's supposed to be arrested," a deputy complained to the *Miami Herald*.

A reporter for *Life* magazine came down after the raid and wrote an article about Everglades City that ran for eighteen pages. It told the story of how pot hauling had come to replace fishing as the town's leading industry and how the town and its people had changed as a result. The writer took the angle that marijuana had made a number of families rather well off compared to their backwater neighbors. Some folks had installed swimming pools behind their mobile homes. But according to the article, pot hauling had also pitted citizens against one another, honest fishermen against outlaw smugglers, native-born against outsider. People were suspicious of one another. The fact that Everglades City and Chokoloskee Island had always been a place for pirates and rum smugglers to hide from the world did not seem to matter. Marijuana was different, people said. Those pot haulers were giving the place a bad reputation. The article's ending neatly summed up the reality about marijuana hauling: "But it goes on. The money—not to mention the geography and the history of Everglades City—make it impossible to stop."

Operation Everglades had stopped some of us, but not all. We smugglers who slipped through the Feds' wide net were determined to continue doing with relative ease what we did so well: smuggle weed and make lots of money.

Some bad movies get a sequel, whether they deserve it or not, and the government's came a year later when Operation Everglades II swept through town in 1984. This time, the Feds were serious. They arrested Darrel, his four brothers, and all of his other key players—a major blow to our operation. They took most of the crewmen who had been involved since the beginning and left in their wake a town of mostly women, wives and girlfriends whose means of support had been hauled away like a boatful of stone crabs. But once again, Clark and I were spared, as were most of the crew who worked in the background. As for Captain Red, he counted his blessings, and with a wink and a tip of his hat, he backed away into obscurity.

Not long after the brothers and what was left of their fugitive crew turned themselves in, an article appeared on the front page of the *Miami Herald*. In bold print it read, "The Cocaine Cowboys of Miami Have Got Nothing on the Daniels Brothers of Everglades City." That headline was completely misleading. The article referred to sheer volume of product being smuggled, but made no mention of the fact that, in our operation, violence was not tolerated and was simply not necessary. In Miami, however, death and destruction were the order of the day. The headline and the article gave a more sinister and sensational portrayal of our operation.

On the other hand, the article's accounting of the Daniels brothers' cumulative wealth and assets was remarkably accurate. Agents seized the following property, all of it allegedly obtained through the Daniels brothers' drug profits: six parcels of land in Collier County, Florida, and more in Tennessee; two condominiums at the Everglades City Club Restaurant and Marina; and an investment in a Netherlands Antilles corporation that also owned Florida land, two airplanes, and four commercial fishing vessels. In addition, 580,000 pounds of marijuana with an estimated street value of $252 million was seized, which brought the total amount of marijuana seized since 1981 to over 750 tons. Other miscellaneous assets—such as cars, sport boats, and vacation properties worth more than $5 million—were also seized.

Operation Everglades may have been a flop, but Operation Everglades II was a pretty major success for the federal government. Indictments and arrests since the summer of 1981 topped 256 people. Darrel, Randal, Sherald, and Dwain turned themselves in to the

Collier County Sheriff's Office in Naples over the next few days after the operation. Then they ultimately ended up in the Tallahassee federal correctional institution. Craig, the youngest brother, whose chiseled features bore a remarkable resemblance to a young Clark Gable right down to the mustache, had suffered an accidental self-inflicted gunshot wound to the upper thigh and later surrendered himself directly to the prison.

While recuperating at his home on Chokoloskee Island, he had walked out into his front yard one day and realized that he was all alone. The only people who meant anything to him were gone. He wrestled with his own personal demons for a brief moment and shook off any regret for being the first who introduced his brothers to pot hauling—they were all big boys. They made their own decisions. In the beginning, the four other Daniels boys turned their backs on Craig. They called him crazy for getting involved with those Cuban fellows they assumed would sooner kill you than pay you. When Craig showed them a suitcase full of cash, they stopped calling him crazy.

"We could all really use this right now," he told his older brothers as he offered them cash. "Hell! Go buy your kids bicycles!"

Darrel and two others caved and took some cash and a job. The third came around after a few days and took an armful of cash and a job as well.

As he recovered from his wound and thought about his brothers languishing in prison for what he had gotten them into, Craig decided to go from one form of rehabilitation to the next. He phoned his longtime friend Floyd B. and asked him to drive him to Tallahassee. Craig arrived on the front steps of his new home, sat down, and waited outside to be reunited with his siblings. Four hours passed before a guard acknowledged Craig's presence with a vague nod.

"Sir, my name is Craig Daniels," he said.

Pausing on the top step, the guard asked, "And what can I do for you, Mr. Daniels?"

"Well," he began, "my brothers Darrel, Randal, Sherald, and Dwain are in there, and I'm here to join them . . . I mean . . . surrender."

With a smug grin and vague look of recognition on his face, the guard said, "So you're one of the Daniels boys, are ya? I'll be right back." The guard disappeared through the heavy white double French doors and abruptly returned with four others to escort Craig into the building. This is where Craig's personal nightmare—and his brothers'—began. Their reunion provided a measure of contentment for each of them, at first. Yet their media-created personas preceded them in the prison yard. Their infamy spread like a disease through the compound. The prison population yielded before them as the brothers strolled the yard. Even Craig, as he hobbled on his crutches, was given a wide berth. But the guards, who did not yield, whispered about the "Everglades Cartel." Those cowardly guards barked obscenities to their faces in an attempt to provoke reactions from the drug-smuggling Daniels "cartel." They were like a crowd of villagers circling defenseless caged tigers and poking them with sharp bamboo sticks. Even the warden knew about the Daniels boys and hated them, especially Craig, who was viewed as the instigator. It was all the media's fault. The press created this image of an "Everglades Cartel" comprised of brothers who were more vicious than the machine-gun-toting "Cocaine Cowboys" in Miami.

None of the brothers earned all that much prison time anyway. Craig received the longest sentence, which he got because he had been in prison before and because the federal magistrate presiding over his case had absolutely no fucking idea how to sentence him or his brothers.

"I have never in all my years come across anybody quite like you people!" he told the brothers. "Mr. Daniels, do you realize that this will be your second time going to prison?"

Looking a bit perplexed himself, Craig answered typically and respectfully, "Yes, sir, I do."

"Well, Mr. Daniels . . ." The magistrate began fumbling with his paperwork, then in a stern voice asked him, "Does five years sound like a long time to you?"

"Yes, sir, it sure does sound like a very long time," Craig replied.

The gavel came down.

"Five years it is!"

The honchos in Tallahassee eventually sent the brothers to different prisons throughout the South, but somehow Darrel, Randal, Sherald, and Dwain all eventually wound up together again at the federal prison camp in Montgomery, Alabama, on Maxwell Air Force Base—affectionately referred to as a Club Fed. They were put to work immediately as block masons, which was work the boys had actually done during southwest Florida's construction boom spawned by the arrival of old Yankees who were moving to the Sunshine State. They worked each day within the boundaries of the enormous base that had no fences or controlled movement. They worked alongside other cons and for air force personnel, not the guards!

Craig, on the other hand, wound up in Indiana at the Terre Haute federal correctional institution, widely considered to be the basement of the federal penal system. Down in Alabama, the air force was in the process of laying a million stone blocks for its expansion of Maxwell AFB, so when the brass heard that another Daniels boy was housed in the federal prison system, they made plans to have him transferred to Montgomery to join his brother stonemasons. The fact that Craig didn't know shit about masonry work was a secret the brothers all kept to themselves. Craig pulled his hitch at the air force base, learning the job one block at a time while bullshitting his way past the US Air Force and the unwitting Bureau of Prisons.

Back in southwest Florida, the pot hauling never stopped. We just eased back the throttles a bit until the heat was off. The Feds had cut off the snake's head, but most of the body was still intact.

In the months that followed the government's second operation, another local smuggler and Cuban friend of mine named Ruben came to see me. With him was a guy named Jorge, a Cuban friend of his from Miami. The raid had taken down some of their usual associates, which caused a backlog of their own inventory. In the absence of Darrel and his brothers, now doing their time up in Alabama, Ruben had come to me for help setting up a job.

I'd done my share of hauling, but I'd never organized a shipment before. That said, after nearly five years of hauling pot I had learned just how easily it could be done. Smuggling was not exactly rocket science. I just had to be willing to take the next big step up the ladder. It might sound strange, but I wasn't apprehensive, worried, or frightened at this prospect of being The Man. It just came naturally to me. After all, it was just another job. A risky job, a profitable job, but a job just the same. My life could change in a big way if I wanted it to.

Jorge asked me straight out: "Can you do this?"

I didn't hesitate. "You bet your ass. I can do anything you want."

First, I had to meet with the big guys in Miami. These were the Cuban boys who were buying the pot from the Colombians. So I went to meet Carlito and Leo. Carlito was a short, chubby guy with an unusual sense of humor. He spoke English very well and was eager to get to work. Leo was tall and slender, and he liked wearing flowered shirts opened in the front to show off the .357 revolver he always had tucked in his pants. He said it made him look like that *Magnum, P.I.* guy on TV.

It disturbed me a little. In all the years I'd been in this business, none of us had ever carried weapons. There was no need. We were just average, everyday guys who knew one another very well and were not violent. We all had talents for which we were paid handsomely—that is, we could navigate the labyrinth of waterways among southwest Florida's Ten Thousand Islands. We could maneuver speedboats and airboats among the mangroves and forests as easily as driving down a street, all in order to avoid those who might be chasing us. With evasive skills like that, nobody needed a weapon for protection.

Leo was obviously taking his part in the Cubans' side of this organization very seriously. But there was also a joking quality to him, in a sarcastic manner. That made him a little hard to figure out sometimes. But don't get me wrong; these guys were serious players.

They were part of the crime wave brought on by the Mariel boatlift in 1980, when thousands of Cubans were told by Fidel Castro that they could just set sail for Florida. Most of the 125,000 refugees who fled Cuba in floating death traps were peaceful people, many of whom would be reunited with long-lost family members in Florida. Many other exiles, however, had just been released from prison or from loony bins by Castro, and now some of these same guys were up to their necks in a war with the Colombians over cocaine trafficking. That war involved killing one another in the streets of Miami for control of the drug trade. I wanted no part of that. I was just a simple pot hauler.

I explained to Carlito and Leo how my end of the operation would work. I described to them the types of hauling boats, radios, chase boats, scanners, and radar we would use. I summarized how we would gather intelligence on all Coast Guard, marine patrol, local sheriff deputies, and highway patrol from Everglades City to Miami. The most important bit of information I provided was the charge for this service. One hundred and forty-five dollars would be paid to me for every pound that was brought from Colombia. Their load would then be delivered to them in Miami.

Up until now I had been involved in every aspect of the work, and I had kept my eyes open and listened to everything the bosses had said. I had to—my ass was on the line the same as everyone else's, and I needed to know this shit. Besides, the Cubans didn't need to know what I knew or didn't know. Recognizing your own limitations is one thing; broadcasting them to your crew can damage your credibility as a leader, and advertising them to your partners can get you killed. So I just went with the flow. The infrastructure for doing the work was already in place; all I had to do to put it back into motion was calculate the pay rate for at least thirty guys and gals, from the handlers and drivers working the shore crew to the boats and their crews working off- and onshore.

That might sound complicated, but it wasn't. It was the perfect illusion because I didn't have a fucking clue what to ask for. I knew that these weren't Wall Street traders I was dealing with. I was never intimidated by these guys. You probably imagine these backroom deals being made by sinister gun-toting drug dealers, but that would be wrong. We made a verbal contract and I gave them a number: the total weight for that first job was to be 27,000 pounds, which meant just over \$3.9 million would be paid to me and my crew for our services. The balance would be theirs—about \$12 million, I figured. During those days, you could buy pot in Colombia for between ten and sixteen dollars a pound, depending on the harvest season, either fall or winter. You could then turn around and sell it in the United States for four hundred and fifty dollars a pound. I informed them that $4 million of their goods would be held by me at a hidden location and would be given back to them upon receipt of payment. This was not negotiable. If they paid in full, I would release the entire amount. If a partial payment was made, I would release an equivalent amount. This was to ensure that we would get paid one way or another, in case they lost the shit on their end.

I also insisted that one of their men be in sight of their merchandise at all times. He would go wherever the ships were being loaded in the Caribbean and count the pieces alongside one of my men. There would be no doubt about how the haul took place and how many bales there were. If we were busted or threatened by approaching Coast Guard or marine patrol and had to toss the shit overboard or get on the chase boat and haul ass, he would have a man there to verify what went down. They were impressed with my knowledge and self-confidence, and the terms were agreed upon. I had seen the planning for this kind of operation a thousand times. I had been on the boats and carried out the orders. Now it was my time to give them.

Nobody on our crew questioned the shuffling of positions and the new hierarchy. We were just service providers, the people who did not own the stuff but were contracted to move it. By proxy, we were working for whomever Carlito and Leo were working for, and very few people knew we were providing the service. It would be silly to think that with all of the shit coming out of South America that we would be the only pot haulers. Of course there were the odd crews here and there all over the country who would contribute their fifteen- and twenty-ton claims to fame, then get ratted out or busted. My hat is off to them. There were also a few guys like myself in South Florida who from time to time would bid against one another for jobs, then share crews to get it done. We were like pot-hauling contractors. It was also common to switch things up by using these other crews when the work was abundant or if we received information on law enforcement activity that caused us to cease activities in our area and decompress for a while. The unique topography of the Everglades coastline and its unforgiving labyrinth of islands allowed it to become part of a way of life that had spanned three generations. We were all just workers. The guys on the boats didn't care where the work was coming from as long as it was still coming.

I asked Carlito and Leo for $60,000 up front to secure boats and key personnel, sort of a good faith gesture on their part. That sounded good to them, on one condition. They asked me if I would go to Colombia for them and inspect their purchase and evaluate its quality, then mark it with my own unique seal of approval.

Of course I would, I told them. They offered to fly me there by private jet, and I could take my friend Ruben, the guy who initiated this deal, with me as translator. It would be safe for him to accompany me because he was only half Cuban. Like I said, these were the days of the Miami cocaine wars when guys were getting killed left and right. Cubans and Colombians didn't trust one another, so they put a gringo, a white guy like me, between them to work the deals. Over the years, our crews would smuggle a little cocaine, but because of the violence, we tended to steer clear. The boys only hauled something like one hundred thousand pounds of coke—which was nothing compared with the amount of pot we hauled. Coke smuggling was too dangerous, and the law gave you a lot more time in prison if you were caught with that shit. The money was way better and the loads were easier to conceal, but it just wasn't worth the risk.

Two days later Ruben and I took a limousine from Naples to Miami, where we boarded the Cubans' private jet and flew south to an undisclosed destination. I really didn't want to know where exactly we were headed. All we knew was that the end of our flight would put us somewhere in the jungle northeast of Cartagena and we would land on a private airstrip owned by "the Boss." (I'm going to refer to him from here on out as the Boss because I respect his anonymity—and I value my life.)

Some in our business considered the Boss second only to Pablo Escobar as the most dangerous drug kingpin on this planet. Let me just say this about Escobar: He was not the king shit like everyone has been told. His ruthlessness is the only thing that earned him his infamous distinction. A woman by the name of Griselda Blanco was the true kingpin. Blanco and her husband brought Escobar off of the streets of Medellin, Colombia, and taught him how to gather the paste and produce and sell the coke. She emigrated to the United States and began using Pablo as a source for her coke, sparking the Miami cocaine wars. Blanco was the true "Queen of Cocaine," the godmother of smuggling, a ruthless woman who approved of the slayings of children and pioneered the use of motorcycle-riding assassins during the 1980s. She spent twenty years in US prisons before being sent back to Colombia, where the papers said she kept a low profile, a good idea if you've ordered the murders of dozens of people and made hundreds of enemies. She was gunned down in 2012 in Bogotá, killed by none other than a pair of gunmen on motorcycles. How appropriate. She was sixty-nine years old.

Anyway, the man I had come to Colombia to do business with was the leader of one of the most notorious drug cartels operating in that country. His position of power and wealth was inherited from his father. We were told that he would be surrounded by loving family and loyal associates—all of whom carried automatic weapons and were sworn to protect him with their lives, if necessary.

Five hours later, as the sun descended on the faraway horizon, we began our own descent through the clouds. As if a magician had pulled a blindfold from our eyes, a vast and beautiful jungle canopy suddenly appeared beneath us. Our landing strip, carved into the jungle floor, guided us as a channel marker would signal a ship sailing on this seemingly endless sea of green. Flying just above the treetops, we held our breaths during the entire white-knuckle approach and landing. We touched down on a well-kept runway, and from there, we took a Ford Bronco a mile up a switchback mountain road, also very well maintained, to the Boss's palatial home. We spent the next two days there, wrapped in the warm caress of the thick equatorial air.

We arrived late in the afternoon. As our hosts would have it, we were not introduced to the Boss that evening. Instead, we were escorted to "an apartment" located in the rear of the house. They called it an apartment, but that didn't do it any justice because the place could have been a house in itself: Three beautiful bedrooms, each with its own full bath, with walk-in showers and water closets, and a living room the size of my entire house back home. A theater room, a full kitchen—it was incredible. We were served a steak-and-lobster dinner in our own dining room. The meal was prepared by the Boss's personal chef.

After dinner we relaxed in a Jacuzzi on the terrace. We were offered female companions, which Ruben accepted willingly and I graciously refused. My preoccupation with business matters and the overwhelming size and beauty of the palace was just a bit intimidating, not to mention that the sounds coming from the other room conjured up memories of me and Lori. Needless to say, I didn't sleep very well that night. I was restless after the day's events and in anticipation of meeting the prince of this palace.

After a long night of tossing and turning, morning came and once again we were served a banquet. This time it was a breakfast buffet that offered up every dish imaginable. We could have anything we wanted. All we had to do was ask.

After breakfast, I met the big guy's right-hand man.

"You can just call me . . . uh . . . Rick." (I took it that his name was not Rick.)

Every Rick I'd ever known was sort of tall and lanky, more tendon than muscle, with a bit of a look of "duhh" in his eyes and mouth. In other words, not too bright. This Rick, on the other hand, was a short fucker, five feet, six inches tall if he was a foot. His hair was down to his shoulders, and as you might expect of a Colombian guy, it was jet-black. I never saw his eyes because he wore sunglasses day and night. He couldn't stand still for two fucking minutes. Just being near the guy gave me a wedgie.

After the introductions, Ruben and I were given a tour of the main house and grounds. It was absolutely extraordinary. The front room had beautiful Spanish-style stone floors, and in the areas where people could gather were marble floors and large plush rugs. Crystal chandeliers hung from the vaulted ceilings rimmed with sculptured crown molding, laced with gold leaf, and the walls were adorned with priceless works of art. Wide, winding stairways curled up and down through rooms, all throughout the house. Some of them led to dead ends. One set wound toward a revolving door, through which a person suddenly found himself standing outside and locked out of the house. Some stairs circled right back to where you started. Being in the house felt like being lost in a magnificent maze. Rick explained that the stairs were built this way because the Boss's father was killed by rebels who had invaded his home a few years earlier. The winding staircases were designed to confuse intruders and give those who lived in the house a means of escape.

How the hell could anyone ever get within a mile of this place, let alone get inside? I thought to myself.

Everyone I'd seen since stepping off the plane carried a weapon of some sort, from automatic rifles to pistols. Even the chef had a 9-millimeter handgun tucked into the back of his pants. Security cameras were everywhere, both in the house and in the jungle that surrounded it. Besides that, the place was lit up with floodlights that could probably be seen from outer space. Did I mention the fountains? I'll be damned if there wasn't a fountain everywhere I turned. I commented on the number of fountains I saw. Rick said, "The sound of the running water makes it virtually impossible to overhear any conversations. So basically, if a business conversation must take place, we move next to a fountain."

Just another typical feature in a typical drug lord's home.

After we toured the house and grounds, it was time to meet the man himself. We adjourned to the living room to wait for him. The place they all called the living room was more like a great hall, and like the rest of the house, it was lavish and comfortable. It was definitely a man's home. The furniture was meant to be used, and it was used well. The stout mahogany-wood-framed and comfortably pleated couches, recliners, love seats, and captain's chairs with matching ottomans were all covered with the softest leather I've ever relaxed upon. The heads of large beasts were hung on the walls, which were also decorated with the softest features of the room, a collection of diverse and wonderfully ornate tapestries and works of art. Light-dampening drapery interlaced with satin and silk unwound from the valances atop the French picture windows and spilled to the floor like shimmering waterfalls, creating a scene of animals wailing silently in an imaginary jungle. The room was a marriage of beauty and death.

A few minutes later our host entered. He wasn't at all what I had expected. His intimidating reputation had painted a picture in my mind of a menacing, monstrous, murderous kingpin. But this guy turned out to be an ordinary-looking fellow in his midforties. A bit overweight, although he carried the pounds well. His long black hair was pulled back into a ponytail, and he wore a loose-fitting T-shirt over his husky frame. Printed on the front was a smiley face, and underneath it read, "HAVE A NICE DAY." As he walked past us to accept a glass of iced tea offered by Rick, I saw that on the back of this shirt was a smoking pistol, a smiley face with a hole in its head, and the words "OR ELSE." The T-shirt was a fitting complement to his camouflage pants, held up by a belted sidearm, and the jungle-style combat boots he wore on his feet. He didn't speak a lick of English, but he was not at a loss for words. As he turned and approached me, he was laughing and speaking Spanish with arms held out. He hugged me, greeting me as if we'd known each other for years. He sure was a jolly fellow. I guess I'd be jolly, too, if I was worth several billion dollars. I didn't understand a word he was saying, but that's why my pal Ruben was there.

"Welcome to my home. I hope you were comfortable," Ruben translated.

"Yes, we were, and you're a very attentive host," I said.

He told me how he had always wanted to visit America, and I suggested a few hot spots on South Beach in Miami. He laughed.

"If I want to get shot at," Ruben translated, "I could just visit Cartagena."

We enjoyed a big laugh, and I cocked my mouth to one side and whispered to Ruben, "All he has to do to get shot at is step outside his own front door."

After chatting and sharing a few more laughs and a few more glasses of iced tea, it was time to get down to business—sort of. "Let's go sample some of my product," the Boss said. He walked out the door, yelling, "I'll drive!"

As we exited the house, Rick handed each of us a fully automatic AK-47 assault rifle. We climbed into the Boss's Bronco for a half-hour ride through the jungle. Accompanying us were two bodyguards who carried their own automatic rifles. We came to a spot in the jungle that was relatively clear, though the tropical canopy obscured the view from above.

As soon as Rick opened his door, the sweet smell of Colombian Red smacked me in the face. I closed my eyes, tilted my head back, and deeply inhaled the intoxicating scent. Stepping out of the truck and slinging the AK-47 over my shoulder, I followed our new friends into the tangle of vines and branches. I pushed the branches and their large thick leathery leaves from my face as we made our way across the jungle floor.

Then, it appeared right in front of me like an ancient Incan ruin. The bales, which resembled giant blocks of stone, were neatly stacked in six long rows that measured roughly fifty feet long by twenty feet wide, and towered twelve feet above our heads. As we walked among these false ruins, I had become pleasantly distracted by the sounds of the jungle. Birds of all kinds sang a different part of the same song. Hundreds of crazy little spider monkeys swung on the branches of the canopy above my head. They jumped from tree to tree and performed a perfectly choreographed dance to the song the birds sang. For a moment I dreamed in slow motion. Then a voice in my dream called out.

"Here, take this."

When Rick touched my arm, it was as if he had punched the off button on my own personal stereo. I was at once back in focus and back to business.

Rick handed me a bamboo shaft about two inches in diameter and eight feet in length. Attached to one end of it was a piece of PVC pipe with the end cut off at an angle, like the end of a giant hypodermic needle. The pointed end was used to stick bales at random, then twisted to extract a sample of the contents for my inspection. I used the Boss's personal pipe to sample the taste and potency of each little bit that was taken. The long pole allowed me to reach the bales at the top of the stack. As we made our way down one row and up another, sampling the bales, Ruben translated back and forth between the Boss and me. I praised the quality of his product and the neat and efficient way it had been packaged, and I asked him to explain the process. I knew the product was first compressed into tight blocks, each weighing about sixty pounds. That was great because it made them easier to handle. The blocks were wrapped in black plastic, bound tightly with duct tape and sleeved in burlap. Then the open end was stitched closed. I had seen this type of packaging before, having been on the receiving end of many shipments, but what I wanted to know was how the process began.

The Boss explained that the plants were brought from the fields by pack mules. Then the marijuana was stripped of excess stems and spread out over chicken wire framed in two-by-fours, which allowed the dried leaves—the shake—from the buds to fall through. It was then compressed by ordinary household trash compactors that were powered by several generators hidden in the jungle behind us. Everything was done under the cover of a large green canvas structure that resembled the big top at a circus. That not only helped conceal the merchandise but also kept the monsoons from damaging it before it could be packaged.

Nothing in that jungle factory was built to be permanent. It was all designed to be broken down and transported at a moment's notice, like an army on the move. If his stash was discovered by the local police or military, the Boss would have to pay them in order to keep it. If that happened, his men would need to move it to another location. Otherwise, he would have to pay again and that would drive up the price of his product. My associates were paying sixteen dollars per pound, but if the price did go up another five or ten dollars, they really wouldn't have given a shit. They were still going to make millions.

Let me explain the math of this kind of transaction, which is capitalism in its purest form. A purchase of 27,000 pounds of marijuana required an initial investment of $432,000. When the merchandise reached the United States, the resale of that much weed ballooned the value of your investment to $12,150,000, from which my fee of $3,915,000 was deducted. As in any market, big risk means big profit.

I was satisfied that what I had sampled was worth every dime. Now came the time to mark and weigh each bale so I would know that what I sampled was what I would receive. Marking bales had become routine years earlier so that the many working smugglers in Florida could identify which load from Colombia was theirs. In the old days, only a few dudes hauled. Eventually, Darrel, Craig, and Sherald led their own operations and sometimes their crews would unload the wrong ship. So many marijuana boats were stacked up offshore it looked like it was a fucking parking lot. The crew managers all knew one another, so they worked out whose shit was whose later. As the jobs grew in number and sheer size, however, it became important to mark your bales so that you got your proper load—and payday. Marking and weighing the bales took the rest of the day, until just after nightfall.

Hot and sweaty, our skin stained brown with resin dust from the weed, we finished marking the bales and went back to the house to clean up, have something to eat, and relax. After a long warm shower and a thirty-minute sauna in our own private bathrooms, Ruben and I checked out the theater. There were a dozen recliners arranged in a semicircle, and on the table next to each was a bag of coke. The movie we chose to watch was *Scarface*. This Al Pacino cult classic had come out a couple of years earlier, and I know that it was a bit of a cliché, but it was remarkably appropriate for the venue. We poured ourselves drinks and cut up our names in coke before snorting it. Then we sat back and watched Tony Montana get his ass shot up.

After the movie, Ruben and I strolled along a cobblestone path among the trees and plants of a garden that grew in the middle of the house. The path led us to a set of huge French doors. We opened them and met with the Boss in his dining room, where we sat down to a dinner fit for a kingpin. I didn't usually drink, but the giant cocaine rails had killed my appetite, so I downed about five whiskies neat to kill the buzz just so I could eat. I could tell it was going to be a long night.

After dinner we adjourned to the living room, or, as I thought of it, the great hall. We were greeted by Rick, the two bodyguards, and two dozen other men who had assisted us in weighing and moving bales earlier that day. We were also joined by two to three dozen beautiful women, who mingled around us. Everyone was laughing, talking, drinking, and smoking weed and cigars. A giant bowl of cocaine sat on the bar like a candy jar, available to whoever wanted a snort—which was everybody in the room, including the Boss.

As the night wore on, Ruben and I settled into a coke-fueled conversation with the king of this castle. We talked about how we came to be where we were at that moment, and about our families. Family was very important to him, he told us. Although I was still a bit young to have a family, I explained to him that at that point in my life, having a family probably wasn't a good idea. He understood and told me that at his age, regardless of the business he was in, it was important for him to have a family and, even more important, to keep them close.

I was the guest of honor, and he was the host of a party that surely his family, especially his wife, would not have approved of. We were told that on the day we arrived his wife and the kids had gone to visit her mother and father, presumably for the duration of our visit. The drugs she wouldn't have minded. That was more or less an accepted lifestyle. But not the women. Beautiful, exotic women. They weren't here just for show; they were here for pleasure, and the pleasure was taking place all over the house.

The party went on, and so did the conversation with the big guy. He was relaxing in his La-Z-Boy recliner when a guy whom I did not recall having seen before strolled into the room. He walked up to the Boss and whispered something in his ear. A strange look formed on the Boss's face. His smile was replaced by a look of surprise, then absolute terror. His eyes bugged out as he leaped from his chair and ran toward the kitchen. I followed hot on his heels. He ran down the hallway, through the kitchen, and out the back door, where he paused to take a quick look around to make sure the coast was clear. Then he took off down a winding stairway, across a veranda, and down another set of escape stairs. He sprinted across the backyard and into the jungle, with me right on his ass throughout. About twenty feet in, he stopped and hit the ground like a commando, as if he were ducking incoming fire.

I ran another hundred feet or so, then dived into the bushes like a swimmer from the starting block. My heart was beating a mile a minute. I lay there for what seemed like an eternity. I was out of breath and being eaten alive by mosquitoes the size of dragonflies. I had escaped a few close calls in my time in the Gulf of Mexico, dodging the Coast Guard, federal agents, and the local yahoos, but I had never once been this freaked out. Now, facedown in a South American jungle, I was absolutely terrified. I didn't know what the Boss had heard, but I knew that I was about to find myself in the middle of a shoot-out between Colombian drug cartels. In the silence of the jungle, I realized something: I was the only son of a bitch who had run out of the house with the Boss. Had I been lucky to escape with him and not run down one of those fucked-up staircases? Were we sitting ducks all by ourselves in the jungle? Or was it all just a ruse to get me out of the house so he could put a bullet in my skull? I didn't move or make a sound.

From where I lay, I could just make out the back of the house lit up by floodlights. I kept my head down and my eyes open. I could neither see nor hear anyone or anything moving in front of me. One of the Boss's men began yelling something from the rear of the house. I figured that if there was going to be a shoot-out, it would have started by now, but nothing was happening. I could not understand what the guy was yelling about, but whatever it was drew a hearty laugh from the Boss. My last nerve was nearly fried.

"What the fuck's going on?" I mumbled.

I saw the Boss through the shadows of the trees, a bulky silhouette against the floodlights. I watched him rise and start to make his way out of the jungle and back toward the house. Cautiously and reluctantly, I stood up and did the same.

I brushed away the bugs, leaves, dirt, and other jungle crap from my skin as I entered the house. I walked into the living room and stopped dead in my tracks. The party had not skipped a beat, and the big guy was back in his chair, sweating profusely. Rick handed him a fresh drink. The Boss reclined, saw me, and started laughing so hard that I thought his big belly would explode. One of the women translated what he was saying to me.

"Where in the hell did you think you were going?" he asked.

I just stared at him, stone-faced, then scanned the rest of the crowd.

"Well, when the big dog gets up, throws his drink on the floor, and hauls ass out of the fuckin' house, my ass is following him!" I said.

Everyone in the room started to laugh.

"Does somebody want to tell me what the fuck is so funny?" I said, still more than a little shocked and confused.

Everybody in the room but me had found out that it was a false alarm. A message had come up the mountain from his men stationed along the roads below that the Boss's wife was on her way home. When the message reached the big man, he freaked out and high-tailed it out of the house. He knew that a party with twenty-some whores in attendance would, at the very least, put him in the shit-house with his wife. He couldn't have her find out about the party because he did not want her to have a reason to leave him. He simply could not afford for that to happen, partly because of love and partly because of business. If she did decide to leave him, one of two things would happen. He would either have to kill her or let her leave. She knew too much about him and his business for him to let her go, and he couldn't bring himself to kill the mother of his children. So, when confronted with the news that his wife was headed up the mountain, he chose to get the hell out of the house and hide in the jungle and let Rick and the others get bitched out for having a party. They would tell her that her husband was taking care of business elsewhere, therefore leaving him unaccountable for the tropical orgy unfolding in her home.

I couldn't wrap my head around it. Here was a guy who was the head of his own cartel, worth several billion dollars. He'd dealt with some of the most dangerous people on the planet every day, had probably ordered a few of them killed or had put a slug or two in them himself, and yet he turned into a big chickenshit pussy when he thought his wife was going to bust his balls over a party. Go figure.

Turned out, it wasn't even his wife who had come to the house. It was some other party guest.

After it was all explained to me, I laughed with them as they laughed at me, but I thought to myself, *Fuck this shit. It's time to go home.*

The next morning we prepared to leave. The housecleaning staff had done their job, and so when his wife actually came home, she never knew a thing. Ruben and I said our good-byes and good lucks to the Boss. He slapped his hand on my shoulder and invited me to come back and visit him again. He told me that he thought I was a funny guy and that's what this business needed, more guys with a sense of humor. I told him I would love to come back again (and I did, one or two dozen more times).

Traveling back down the mountain road, Ruben and I descended through a layer of clouds that appeared to be resting on the treetops. I remarked about how mysterious and beautiful this country was. Everything was so bright, moist, and colorful. The jungle was a living, breathing organism. At the airstrip, under that layer of clouds, we boarded our jet for our return flight to Miami. The pilot taxied out onto the runway. Without stopping, he pushed the engines to full throttle, and the g-forces fused me to the seat. Within seconds, we were off the ground and engulfed in a shroud of mist. I watched little droplets swiftly jerking up and down while streaking across my window. It was like an EKG recording the rhythm of my heartbeat. Surprisingly, we broke through the top of the clouds, and the morning sunrise kissed my face as the jet banked hard to the right. The pilot's voice came over the intercom, apologizing for the abrupt takeoff but insisting it was necessary in order to clear the mountain just to our left. I glanced over at my pal Ruben, and he looked at me with big wide eyes and pointed his finger at the window next to him. I leaned over and caught a close-up view of the mountaintop we had barely avoided. We were still climbing as I leaned back in my seat and tried to relax. My first trip to Colombia was behind me. I had partied with a druglord and made a multimillion-dollar deal, and now the pressure was off. Now, all I had to do was plan for a ship to go back and pick up our merchandise.

CHAPTER TEN

When I got back to the States, I immediately began making preparations. I met with my pal Johnny in Everglades City, whose job it was to round up the shore crew and to discuss what needed to be done. We would send a shrimp boat to Colombia and have it loaded with the bales that bore my subtle, but distinctive, mark. From there, the boat would make an eight- to ten-day journey north through the gap between the Yucatan Peninsula and Cuba, then continue on northeast, toward the southern tip of Florida. The captain would contact me when he got close, and we'd meet at a predetermined spot just thirty miles off our coast.

From there I would do what I knew best: I would send two crab boats, accompanied by our chase boat, to unload the bales. Unloading a ship wasn't always as simple as pulling alongside and waiting for the load to automatically pour down onto our decks. Most of the time, my guys would jump onboard and climb down into the bowels of the mothership to assist its crew in humping the bales up on deck before the off-load could begin. We each took turns below working in the heat of the still-running engines as we moved that weed. Like a bucket brigade, we passed bales up to a man standing on a pyramid of pot so that the guys on deck could reach down and grab them. We would unload this shrimp boat offshore because it would be suspicious for it to be any closer to the coast due to its size. My crab boats were smaller, and their day-to-day work routine of going out into the Gulf and returning to shore would not attract attention.

When the two loads reached the shore, the plan was for my crew and me to transfer them onto smaller, faster boats, usually mullet skiffs. A mullet skiff is a small net boat used to catch the common baitfish from which the craft gets its name. These skiffs travel at high speeds through shallow water. Mixed in with them would be T-Craft and Morgan boats with center or rear consoles. These smaller, faster boats had a lot of deck space and were equipped with twin 235-horsepower Evinrude motors that were capable of accelerating their sleek vessels from zero to sixty in seconds. The number of boats we used typically ranged from about ten to fifteen. Each made as many trips as needed back and forth to the island until the off-load was completed and the load was stashed safely in someone's house on the island. Picture it if you can: every room in a house stacked floor to ceiling with bales of pot.

Our load would be taken the next day across the causeway to Everglades City, where the road becomes the lone route out of town and meets US 41, the old Tamiami Trail, which stretches from Naples to Miami.

Or at least, that was the way it should have worked. This time it didn't.

Based on what I heard over the radio from our spotters crouched in the bushes along the roadways, there was an unusually high number of sheriff's deputies and what appeared to be unmarked police vehicles out across the causeway. With these guys roaming between Everglades City and Chokoloskee Island, I was hesitant to bring our shipment to shore to the designated house. It wasn't uncommon for the sheriff to pick a night to let us all know that he was still around. Every now and then the law of averages caught up with us and we unexpectedly clashed with the sheriff. We needed to lie low for a little while. But we couldn't just leave the bales on our boats, waiting for the Coast Guard like sitting ducks. So together we decided to take them to a secluded spot among the islands known only to a few of us. We would stack the bales in large blocks, then try to transport them the next night. The spot I had in mind was about three miles south of Chokoloskee, hidden in a mangrove forest within the maze of the Ten Thousand Islands.

When I got there, accompanied by twenty of my crew, we waded into the forest. Unlike our pirate predecessors, who brought out their shovels to bury their booty, we began breaking down dead trees and branches. This needed to done because there was no dry ground in the area. So, working together, we built eight platforms on which to rest the bales. We then formed a line from boat to platform and passed the bales man to man, stacking them about fifty to a platform. It was hard, physical work, complicated by the fact that each boat had to make two trips out and back. There we stood, many of us up to our waists in water and mud, being eaten alive by mosquitoes.

Six hours later, with the sun about to rise, we'd finished. We were dead tired. I headed back to my home to get cleaned up, rested, and prepared for the next night's work in just a dozen hours.

All the suspect traffic the night before had me concerned. I concluded that we still couldn't bring the bales to the stash house. It was too risky. My guys and I devised a new strategy. It was decided that we'd use pitpans, shallow drafting watercraft similar to john-boats, about sixteen feet long and seven feet wide. When loaded with bales, pitpans could float in as little as twelve inches of water. Boats of this type were especially useful at times like this because our new plan was to take the load up the Turner River, through the shallow backwaters of a mangrove forest. We would follow the river until we reached a spot where it flows under US 41, effectively bypassing Chokoloskee Island and Everglades City altogether. From there the bales would be packed into three big box trucks, then taken directly to Carlito and Leo in Miami. As agreed, I would keep a number of pieces in reserve to secure our payment. Those would be loaded into vans equipped with air bag suspension and taken thirty miles away to a close friend's house in the Golden Gate Estates a few miles east of Naples.

So that night, in a fleet of more than a dozen pitpans, we went back into the forest to reclaim our booty. We re-formed our lines to each platform and passed our treasure once again from man to man, restacking the bales safely on the decks of our dry boats.

When that part was completed, we snaked our way through the backwaters to the mouth of the river. Along the way, one of our many spotters hiding out along the route broke radio silence.

"There's a party of fishermen camping on Rabbit Key."

Rabbit Key is one of the small outer islands that we had to go right by in order to get into the pass. Anyone there would have heard the unmistakable sound of a fleet of powered boats passing in the middle of the night. We couldn't afford to draw that kind of attention. These inconvenient campers left us with no choice: we'd have had to shut down our engines and paddle the boats, all eighteen of them, single file past those fishermen.

We were fewer than fifty yards away as we drifted by them on the evening tide. Keep in mind that we were now trying to move 27,000 pounds of pot, without the help of engines, through a maze of islands without being seen or heard, in the blackness of night. We could hear the campers laughing and having a good time. We could see them in the light from their campfire.

That same campfire made it impossible for them to see us in the darkness. They never knew about the multimillion-dollar flotilla passing by them, a stone's throw away. An onshore breeze blew in our favor. It sent the smell of all that pot into the forest and not into the campers' faces. Twenty-seven thousand pounds of pot gives off a very thick and powerful odor with the distinctive hint of burlap. It's not like you're carrying a dime bag in your pocket, if you know what I mean.

We made it past the jolly campers, then restarted our motors and continued the journey to the mouth of the Turner River. As we wound our way through the thick mangrove forest and at times pushed ourselves along with paddles, our caravan of boats was right on schedule. The water was very shallow in the upper part of the river near the highway. I had planned this expedition to coincide with high tide, so we were able to push our boats through.

It took seven hours to arrive, but all of the pitpans made it to the trucks parked near a span of US 41, where the loading immediately began. The first truck took about forty minutes to fill and send off. The second truck took a little less time. We were finding our rhythm. The driver of the third and last truck backed into position, turned off his motor, and then jumped out to help. Approximately twenty minutes into loading that truck, a car pulled over at the end of the bridge that spans the river right next to where we were standing with the weed. My heart rate accelerated, and I think I might have even peed my pants a little—I'm not sure.

"Shit," I said to Johnny. "Who the hell could that be?"

I had men stationed at ten-mile intervals all the way to Miami, spotting for law enforcement of any kind. They would have contacted me over the radio if a cop were headed our way. But this guy wasn't driving anything marked. He had passed all my spotters only to stop right here next to us. We immediately stopped loading and prepared to haul ass out of there. This guy wasn't alone either. When he opened his door to get out, I could see another passenger illuminated by the dome light. Seeing that it was a woman, I knew that this guy wasn't a cop because there were basically no female officers in our neck of the woods in those days. Our truck was backed up to the river behind a few trees and bushes, and our boats were lined down the riverbank, and we were at least thirty yards from the bridge. So unless he could see in the dark and knew right where to look, he wouldn't know we were there. Everyone just stayed quiet and alert, waiting for the guy's next move.

He got out of his car and walked over to our side of the bridge. He looked up and down the road, then unzipped his fly and proceeded to take a piss over the guardrail. Of all the places along this fucking road through the Everglades to stop and take a leak, he picked this one, just a hearty piss stream away from a truckload of Colombian marijuana. He did his business, zipped up, then got back into his car, and just like that the couple drove off. We were no strangers to close calls, but still, we breathed easier once they were several miles down the road. It was my guess that they must have been visiting someone nearby or my guys surely would have spoken up. We then finished loading the truck. The hard part of the job was finally done. We had transported the load from Colombia to the Florida mainland. Now, all we had to do was drive the trucks to the other coast and get paid.

The next day, I went to Miami to meet up with Carlito and Leo, then weigh in the haul and collect the money. Until then, my getting paid for a job had always meant receiving a paper bag filled with cash from a boat captain. This time would be quite different. This time it would be *a lot* more money, and it would be paid out to a lot of other dudes.

First, I had to collect our crew's cut. After the load was weighed, the total payment came to $3,915,000. We went from a horse barn near Homestead, Florida, where the pot was stashed, to Carlito's house in the Miami suburb of Coral Gables. The cash was there. Carlito's home was fairly modest—four bedrooms and three bathrooms. I walked through the front door and was greeted by Carlito's brother and four other guys I didn't know or care to know. All I wanted to do was collect my money, get home, and finally be done with this job.

Getting paid wasn't as easy as it sounds. First, you actually had to count all of the $3,915,000. Leo had two money-counting machines that were a big help. Carlito and I sat down at the dining room table and began counting. The ten-dollar bills were in a pile in one bedroom, and the twenties, fifties, and hundreds were each in their own respective rooms. The five-dollar bills were kept in the garage because there were so damn many of them. (Thankfully, there were no one-dollar bills.) Judging by the size of the piles of cash, I knew there was more than just my money in those rooms.

Two of the guys I did not know brought to the table and dumped from their shirts bundles of hundred-dollar bills bound with rubber bands. Carlito and I pulled off the rubber bands and stacked the bills, $10,000 per bundle. We fired up the counting machines and the totaling began. We counted and agreed on totals all night and into the next morning. When the sun rose we had only gone through the hundreds and the fifties. We still had $1,900,000 to count and three rooms and a garage full of cash to go through. Payment was a mix of all denominations because no one wanted to get stuck with all of the smaller bills. That's why everyone had to take their share of fives. The stacks of bills were heavy, and they took up a lot of room. The counting continued throughout the day. As we counted twenties, tens, and fives, the process slowed considerably. When evening rolled around again, we had been counting money now for at least twenty-four hours straight.

Carlito sent his brother to get some cocaine so everyone could stay awake. Thirty minutes later he returned with five ounces of the shit. Everyone dug in and started doing lines. Everyone but me, that is. I would wait until the money was counted because cocaine made me paranoid as hell. Besides that, once I got started, I kept doing it for days until I was sick of it. I didn't want to get messed up while millions of dollars were at stake.

But that didn't stop the other boys. They snorted line after line. The lines grew bigger and bigger, and so did their paranoia. It wasn't long before they were all tweaking, acting paranoid as hell and peering out the windows. The drug had convinced them all that they saw people outside watching us from behind that bush and that tree or that house. But there was nobody out there. I knew better—it was just the coke. When I was high on coke, I used to wish that my clothes were made of the same material as the curtains. That way, I could stand in a window and watch for people and no one would know I was there.

They became so paranoid, delusional, and unfocused that I had to count the rest of the money myself. Carlito came over from time to time to look at the totals and snort a line about six inches long. Fatigue set in, but I guess having all that cash in front of me and the fact that I just wanted to get the hell home kept me going.

Twenty-four hours later, after two days and nights, the counting was done. Three million, nine hundred fifteen thousand dollars sat on the table in front of me. It was time to pack my bags with the cash and go home.

Now, I've watched a lot of movies with guys carrying large amounts of cash. A dude just runs around swinging a bag or briefcase over his head with a quarter of a million dollars in it like it's filled with feathers. Bullshit. That much cash is *heavy*. Just one of my seven suitcases held $670,000 in mixed denominations. I had to use both hands to pick the damn thing up. The handle almost broke off as I carried it to the truck.

I made a phone call to my guys who were holding the extra pot I had kept as security.

"Let it all go."

As I left the house, Carlito handed me four ounces of coke.

"Here, take some *yeyo* with you," he said. "Give some to Johnny and the boys and keep some for yourself." I was happy to get out of there. I would be even happier after the two-hour drive home.

The drive was the only time during the entire job that I was truly anxious. That was the last step in the process. I had nearly $4 million and a quarter pound of coke in the truck with me. I wasn't worried about the drugs—I had my crew to pay. Those guys had busted their asses for this cash, and now it was all up to me to get it to them.

"C'mon, Tim, don't make any mistakes." Talking to myself helped to calm my nerves. "Watch your speed and you'll make it. Here . . . let me turn on the radio."

An AC/DC song filled the truck. I was on a "Highway to Hell."

"Yeah . . . that was a good idea."

The drive back with the cash didn't require spotters or a tagalong. If I got pulled, I was going with the cash. But other than passing an occasional highway patrolman, the drive was uneventful. In the end I managed to get everybody paid, and the $970,000 that was left over was mine. Not a bad payday for my first job as boss.

CHAPTER ELEVEN

By now, I was used to being the pot-hauling guy who made multimillion-dollar deals with Cubans and who still had to live with his slightly off-the-wall girlfriend who was always raging about something askew in her *pampered* life. Drug dealers and their clueless girlfriends, the timeless cliché. We were a toxic combination.

I was weed, Lori was alcohol, and money was the flame. Put me together with that flame and I became as soulfully smooth and laid-back as the tasty sound of Steely Dan's "Hey Nineteen." You put that same shit together with Lori and, well, what the hell did you think would happen? She was the propellant. She was alcohol.

Each time I made some cash, the routine was to celebrate together in our own way. After the deal with the Cubans, a bit of chillin' seemed just the ticket. When you've got the kind of money that I had become used to having, throwing a last-minute trip together didn't require much planning. When Lori and I decided to pack a bag and head for Atlanta to do some shopping, the only question we asked ourselves was how much cash to take with us. Of course that all depended on how much crap we wanted to bring home. Taking tens of thousands of dollars on a vacation was nothing out of the ordinary. We would take short unplanned trips to Atlanta to shop, Atlantic City to gamble, and Montreal or Winter Park, Colorado, to ski. We often hopped in *Pair A Dice* and headed for a resort in the Keys for days at a time. Money bought a lot of freedom.

Money presented its own unique problems, too. Jimmy Buffett wrote my favorite song, titled "A Pirate Looks at Forty," in which he sings about a middle-aged pot hauler who "made enough money to buy Miami" and pissed it all away. That says it all. You've got to spend it. You can't let all that money pile up. You've got to do something with it. Anything.

I once made the mistake of stashing a half million dollars in my attic. About a month later, I climbed back up there to stash some more only to find that mice, little fucking mice, had chewed up about a quarter of a million dollars in hundreds. They had made themselves a nice little house out of it. Sure, I was pissed, but what the fuck could I do about it? I was almost relieved because the money was coming in so fast, I didn't know what to do with it all. When you know you're going to make more, lots more, it's just a waste of your time to let little shit like that bother you. Besides, I had given that much and more away to friends.

I did just what that song said: piss it away or give it away; otherwise I would run out of room to hide it. If you bury it, it gets moldy. If you put it in your attic, rodents eat it. I had a condo near Marco Island before I bought my first house. The vents were packed so full of cash that the air-conditioning system didn't work.

As usual, and right on time, another money-counting session at Carlito's was arranged and I took off to Miami for a few days to collect more cash. The money was becoming a very real pain in the ass. The jobs were coming and going so frequently that I was having a hard time managing the responsibility of buying weed and counting money—especially during Colombia's fall harvest season, when our crew's total monthly pay from an average of four jobs would easily surpass $40 million. So much money was being passed around, I had people being paid very well to whom I could delegate responsibility. There was no way one guy could do all of this, and that's what made this machine work so well. Every layer of the operation was manned by crew members who had a special talent for that particular phase. Some were masters of multiple phases. Thankfully, the matter of trust was never an issue among us, and these delegates were in a much better position to divvy up the pay throughout the layers once I had retained my cut. The majority of the crew didn't know whose job was whose, and frankly they didn't want to know or didn't give a shit as long as they were getting paid.

We made more money than we could count. Our solution to ending those life-sucking hours wasted counting stacks of bills was to simply *weigh* them. We knew from just fucking around with a set of balance beam scales that every bill, no matter what denomination, weighed a gram, and the rubber band holding the bundles of bills together weighed two grams. It turned out to be infinitely faster because it was just a matter of doing a little simple math. I just had to pay attention to the bills as I fanned through them with my thumb to ensure that they were all the same denomination. Then, I counted the bundles as I tossed them into the basket on the scales to keep track of the total number of bands. For example, $1 million in twenties weighed 106 pounds after I subtracted the weight of all those rubber bands. It was that simple.

However, when the count got close to finishing, Leo or Carlito inevitably sent one of their cousins for a celebratory quarter pound of coke, and our breezy system deteriorated. Then it didn't matter how fast the count went because everybody would start tweaking out before it was done.

Once again I was left sitting in the kitchen finishing the count when, from the living room, Carlito quietly asked, "How much we got left, Timmy?"

Knowing that I could see him from where I was sitting, I said, "Just a little under three hundred thousand, my man."

Turning his head ever so slightly, and without taking his eyes off whatever tree or bush in the front yard the cops were supposedly crouching behind, he said, "I have a house in the Bahamas I've been kind of wanting to sell. I think I'd like to move to St. Martin, on the French end. Are you interested?"

"How much do you want for it?"

And once again without removing his gaze from the window, he said, "How much did you say you had left to count?"

Nothing more needed to be said. Thanks to Carlito's impatience, a little coke-fueled paranoia, and the casual nature of our business, I became the owner of a furnished three-bedroom, three-bathroom home with an attached garage and a large swimming pool in the backyard for a little less than three hundred grand. Other properties in the Caribbean would come into my possession over time, but this one was so close to home that it made for a perfect spot to launder a little money. After all, the Britannia and the Paradise Towers casinos were literally just outside its front door.

Needless to say, I didn't waste any time checking the place out or doing a walk-through.

In the summer of 1986 Lori and I decided to take our crazy-ass friend Moose and his fiancée with us to visit the new house, which was on Paradise Island, just across a short bridge from the Port of Nassau. The trip was a wedding present for them, all expenses paid.

We arrived at the airport in the heart of Nassau, collected our baggage, and climbed into one of the dozen or two taxis that were lined up and down the curb out front. When I gave the taxi driver our destination and twenty bucks, he immediately took off, throwing us back in our seats. We all had a white-knuckled grip on the person sitting next to us as we flew down the main drag and out of Nassau.

The Bahamas are one of the most beautiful island chains in the world. Thick tropical vegetation was everywhere, and the white sand beaches were some of the most beautiful I had ever seen. The water was so crystal clear that boats appeared to be floating in thin air.

My mind wasn't on the beach, though. I was trying to figure out if the Bahamian cabdriver was going to get us to the house alive. We sped down a narrow two-lane road at about fifty-five miles per hour. Traffic was bumper to bumper in our lane and bumper to bumper speeding past us in the opposite lane. The driver was in his element, honking his horn continuously, as was every other car on the road. This was how drivers on this little marble in the Caribbean communicated.

Beep, beep! *Fuck you!*

Honk, honk! *Fuck you, too!*

They drive in the Bahamas the same way they drive in England, on the left side of the road, which to us was ass backward. Everyone on the road seemed to be in a big hurry, and everyone seemed to have been taught to drive by the same crazy son of a bitch. They probably passed this shit down from generation to generation. Some old Bahamian fucker sitting in the flittering light of a beachside campfire with his balls hanging to the sand, chanting from the only driving book left on the island. These drivers darted out into other lanes and swerved back just in time to avoid head-on collisions. They played a split-second game of chicken to see if the coast was clear to pass the other crazy son of a bitch in front of them.

As many times as I visited the Bahamas, I never got used to the drivers. You never get used to having the shit scared out of you. We reached that familiar turnabout with the statue of a giant crawfish in its center. It was a monster of a thing standing at least ten feet tall, twenty feet long, made of welded pieces of metal that stuck out all over and was painted to look like a spiny lobster. Three-quarters of the way around the circle and we were headed over the bridge to Paradise Island and home.

When we arrived, we all piled out of the back of the taxi, feeling like we had just won first place in a road rally. I tipped the driver another twenty bucks on top of his fare, and he shot me back a big-ass grin.

"Tanks for da tip, mon!"As I turned to walk away, he added, "I got me a bit of virgin bud, mon. Are ya interested?"

"Oh yeah, my man! I could use a good smoke. After your little sprint from the airport, my ass is puckered up the size of a decimal point."

I did my deal with him and watched as he sped away, turning the corner on two wheels. All of us decided to go for a swim in the pool and relax for a little bit before Moose and I dropped the girls off to do a little shopping at the straw market, where local vendors sold baskets and handmade crafts.

The house had come with a car. It was a 1969 Volkswagen Beetle that appeared to be in pretty good shape. We packed ourselves into the Bug and headed back over the bridge into Nassau and dropped off the girls. Moose and I took off to get stoned and explore the island. We managed to find our way back to the main road, slipping in with the rest of the crazy-ass drivers. Trying to keep up with their pace, we weren't doing too badly until the engine suddenly cut out and the Bug started to lose its momentum. I began pumping the gas pedal in a desperate attempt to breathe life back into our car. That wasn't working. Moose and I looked at each other.

Oh shit.

Cars zoomed and weaved around us as we slowed. Having failed to resuscitate our dying vehicle, we tried to figure out what we should do next. Ahead of us on the right, there was a driveway coming up fast. I had to time our escape from this Hot Wheels track just right. The maneuver would require me to slow down in such a way as to still have enough momentum to cut between two oncoming cars and pull into the driveway. I had only one shot at getting the hell out of everybody's way. I swerved off the road, then saw that the driveway went downhill for about two hundred feet. We skidded to a stop next to an old abandoned plantation home.

We had tears in our eyes from laughing, or maybe we were just happy that we hadn't been killed. Either way, we got out and walked around to the back of the car, where Moose lifted the engine hatch and we immediately saw that the throttle cable had broken completely away from the carburetor. I looked around the property for something we could use as a cable, and I found a worn-out electrical extension cord lying under some bushes. I stripped the plug off one end and the receptacle from the other to make it the perfect length. I twisted the wires on one end of the cord around the throttle assembly on the carburetor. Then Moose ran the cord out from the engine compartment and in through a back window. The plan was simple. Moose would be my throttle man, tugging on the cord to give the engine some gas, while I steered and took the car through the gears. Moose climbed into the back, and I sat in the driver's seat and fired the Bug up. We managed to get it up the hill but had to stop at the top and wait for traffic to clear. This created a problem because the car did not have an automatic transmission. I had to work the clutch and shift while Moose worked the gas. This was no easy task, sitting at the top of a hill. We had to work in sync, with Moose giving the engine just enough gas at the precise moment I let off the clutch. After several near-fatal failed attempts, we managed to get out onto the road. Now all we had to do was drive this piece of shit home.

"Just give it a little bit of gas and hold it steady."

"No problem," Moose said. "I gotcha covered."

He then proceeded to give the cord a tug-of-war-style pull, and we shot out of there like yesterday's burrito. Moose eased up on the gas just long enough for me to shift into second gear; then he yanked the cord again, hard. He did that shit through all four gears. We kept up with the pack pretty good, but the turnabout with the craw-fish in the center was approaching and I just knew it wasn't going to be a pretty sight. I held on and hoped for the best.

"You maniac," I hollered at Moose as he pulled the cord and sped us up. "You're going to get us killed!"

I turned my head just long enough to see him laughing his ass off, the cord in one hand and a big fat joint in the other.

"Pass me that sum-bitch!" I said, and I didn't mean the cord.

I inhaled that virgin Jamaican bud and started coughing so hard, I thought my face was going to explode. I regained my focus and saw that we were going way too fast for the upcoming turnabout. Not only that, the bud we were toking on had us laughing so hard I could barely see the dashboard, let alone the road. When it came time to make the turn—I didn't.

The Bug was on its own and totally out of control. We smashed into the curb and literally flew past that damn crawfish. When the wheels touched down, we'd spun 360 degrees, then skidded out into the road, throwing grass everywhere. We wound up on the other side of the turnabout, only now we were facing traffic. True to his form, my throttle man gave the cord another tug speeding us the wrong way around the circle. When we got to our turnoff, I cut a hard left and went onto the bridge, still traveling in the wrong lane. Moose let up on the gas, which allowed us to coast down to the other side of the bridge. Thank God the house wasn't too far from the base of the bridge. We plowed through gears one more time, and at the last second I pulled up smartly on the hand brake. Our Bug did a four-wheel drift into the driveway, and we skidded to a stop right in front of the garage. Still laughing uncontrollably, I opened the door, a cloud of reefer smoke rolled out, and then I fell out with Moose right behind me.

We picked ourselves up off the ground and walked to a bike shop, where we bought two mopeds. This was more like it and far less dangerous. My life was now in my own hands as we investigated the island.

Moose and I spent the next few hours cruising down back roads and stopping to take in the beautiful scenery, taking in a few hits off of a joint in the meantime. When we got back to the straw market to pick up the girls, the first thing they said to us was, "Where in the hell have you two been?"

We started talking at the same time, telling our own version of the last few hours until the girls cut us off.

"Do you think you can get us back to the house without killing us?" one of them asked.

He and I shrugged.

We doubled up on the mopeds and headed back to the house for a swim and a joint. Our day was just beginning. Now it was time to hit the casino.

The Britannia Beach Hotel casino was just across the street from the house. I gave Moose and his fiancée a couple of thousand dollars each to get them started, but that didn't last long. Moose had a passion for playing roulette, but he couldn't land on a winning number to save his ass. Half of the spaces on the wheel were black and the other half were red. How fucking hard could it be? But I didn't really care that he was losing thousands of dollars. He was there to have a good time. I, on the other hand, was there for more than just fun and gambling. I had come to Nassau to do a few loads of money laundry. It was easier and a lot more fun there than at home, cooking the books with diving and fishing charters. I changed my "dirty" money into casino chips, then cashed those back out in return for "clean" money. The freshly laundered cash could be declared as winnings when coming through customs on our return trip to the States.

I had numerous opportunities to invest my cash in legitimate enterprises. Friends and friends of friends approached me all the time with their ideas for "the next big thing," but like everything else in life, these were all a crapshoot. Some years back I had considered investing in a very dear friend's dream of becoming a professional wrestler. I loved him like a brother, but I knew that he would probably just take the cash and piss it away on one hell of a party. So my good friend Scotty went on without me and found his backer. He worked hard and became a champion. He was the world heavyweight champ of Extreme Championship Wrestling and a two-time World Championship Wrestling World Tag Team champ under the name of Bam Bam Bigelow, the "Beast From The East." He sported trademark flaming tattoos on his head, and he blustered his way down the aisle and into the ring jamming to Guns N' Roses' "Welcome to the Jungle." The guy made a mint pile-driving bodies into the mat. Who knew?

My game was craps. I loved to roll them bones and did all night while my cohorts got wasted. Like at all of the finer gaming establishments, as long as you're gambling, the drinks are on the house. My pal Moose took full advantage of the casino's hospitality. At about four in the morning the girls helped me carry him back to the house. We laid him out on a lounge chair by the pool and wrapped him up in a bed sheet so he wouldn't get a chill in the early-morning air. Lying there in his white shroud, he looked like a dead body in need of a burial. So we decided to bury him at sea. The two girls stood at attention and saluted our shipmate as I wheeled him over to the edge of the pool. After a brief moment of silence, I asked God to have mercy on his soul, then committed his body to the depths of that chlorinated abyss. The girls and I were laughing so hard, rolling around on the pool deck, that we forgot to pay attention to the body we had just dumped over the rail into Davy Jones's locker. I dove into the afterworld to retrieve my friend and dragged him out onto the deck. He hadn't stirred in several minutes. I was afraid that we had just drowned the poor bastard. In a panic I tore the sheet from his head so that he could breathe, ripping out two fistfuls of his hair in the process. He was facedown, so I rolled him over and sat on his chest and slapped him across the face so fucking hard I swear the music that had been coming from across the street paused momentarily. He responded to my primitive CPR by opening one eye and smiling at me. He had slept through the whole damn ceremony! He was drunk and stoned and sank straight to the bottom. We could never figure out how the hell he managed not to drown. Maybe he was just too stoned to die.

The next morning during breakfast we laughed about Moose's new bald spots and the bright shiny handprint on the side of his face. He couldn't believe that we had actually subjected his body to such a crude ritual. We told him it was a glorious send-off and that his mother would have been bursting at the seams with pride. And so that others might join us in our mourning, we had taken pictures.

We spent most of that day sleeping off the effects of the night before. I had stayed away from alcohol because it wasn't really my thing, but for the others the Bahamas was hangover central. The alarm clock took three snoozes; then we packed our things and called a taxi for another suicide run back to the airport. It was time to go home.

"Home." The word has such a restful sound to it. It's your sanctuary, where all the craziness disappears—right? In retrospect, home was where I had to reconcile the two worlds I inhabited. If I only knew then what I know now, things might have worked out very differently. But who knew? I was young . . . Hell, we were all young. Young and addicted to adrenaline, living dangerously close to the edge. We were modern-day pirates.

And as for Lori and me, we had a blast together, but we had a shitload of problems, too. Most were caused by drugs, drinking, money, or often a combination of the three. God, she was crazy. And I loved being with her. Once I took her out in a new Jeep that I liked to go mudding in out in the woods. Lori stood up in the passenger seat, grabbed the roll bars, and started hollering, "Let's roll it!" I didn't drink when I met Lori, but over time that all started to change. We partied so hard and so long, I would snort what I could out of an ounce of cocaine, and after a few days I'd chase it with a bottle of Jack Daniel's just so I could kill the buzz and get some sleep before our next job. Lori and I partied, fought, fell asleep, woke up, and partied again. One night in Naples, she and I got into an argument over who should be driving (it should have been neither of us). She climbed in the driver's seat of our new Chrysler LeBaron, fired up the engine, and tried to run me down in the parking lot of the nightclub. She chased me down a bank and across another lot until I ran up a flight of concrete steps. She didn't stop, though. She ran the car into the steps as if she were going to drive straight up the stairs and run me over. I leaped out onto the hood from the top step and pounded it with my fists, too high to feel pain, and stomped on the hood with my boots until the air filter made an impression in the hood. I stood up through a cloud of steam and heard her scream, "My car! My car!" I jumped over the windshield, and as she scrambled for the backseat, I snatched the keys from her hand and drove that fucker home. (Not long after that, I bought her a new car.)

All the while, Lori continued working at the bar. I kept working, too. I continued to act as the intermediary between the Cubans and Colombians. I told Lori during one of the first times we met that I was a pot hauler, but beyond that I never really talked about the job with my girl. It was for her own sake as much as mine. And she wasn't that curious—at first.

But the longer we were together, the more devious she became. She wanted to know more about what I was doing when I disappeared for several days at a time. I couldn't tell her, I said. Our relationship—or, more accurately, our degree of trust—became strained by the unique challenges posed by my profession. Let's just say it: Lori was the jealous type. Her jealousy always seemed to be hiding like a gator just beneath the water, waiting for its prey to approach.

Her attacks were alcohol-fueled, each one more furious than the last. And she started reading some fucked-up books by L. Ron Hubbard that had her claiming she could read minds, have visions—all manner of crazy bullshit.

The relationship became more and more volatile. During one of our famous battles, my quick reflexes saved my ass, but they couldn't save me from a $2,000 sacrifice, as a crystal ashtray went flying past my face and stuck like a dart in a mirrored wall behind me. Lori was coming unglued. I learned that a woman's jealousy can manifest itself in many different ways. I learned that a reasonably intelligent, clever, and devious person could set her sights on any goal—she could claim any pretty, shiny thing if she just set her mind to it.

It all came to a head on another one of her hungover mornings. We had awakened to one of our usual heart-to-heart discussions over coffee. She got real quiet for a moment. Then she fixed those green eyes on me like lasers and started in on one of her bullshit "mind-reading" tricks, only this time she repeated back to me verbatim something that one of my Cuban partners had said to me just the day before when we drove back from Miami. My hair tingled as I recognized the conversation.

L. Ron Hubbard, my ass. I didn't say a word. I just turned, walked outside, and went straight to my car. It didn't take long to find what I was looking for. Hell, she wasn't even smart enough to try to hide that little voice-activated cassette recorder sitting just under the driver's seat. I stormed back into the house and stuck it in her face. I punched the button and played back the conversation, knowing full well that if the recorder had been discovered it could have gotten me killed. I smashed the recorder to pieces with my fist only inches from her face.

For all the fury, I loved her, though. I really did. I was addicted to her. But things were never the same after that incident. I couldn't trust that she wouldn't pull another one of her emotionally driven stunts. If we had been, I don't know . . . ordinary, these snits would have only amounted to a jealous couple's squabble. But my situation was extraordinary. Too much was at stake to allow her any more knowledge of my activities.

For the remainder of our time together she never knew that I continued to work in the Gulf. She never knew about my business dealings with Cubans and Colombians. I could never trust her. Our romance resolved itself like every other good thing in my life did at that time: it came to an abrupt end.

CHAPTER TWELVE

I dealt the first hand and told George it was his turn to give me the details on how his ass wound up in prison. He took a deep breath, puffed his cheeks like a bullfrog, and let the story roll out like oxygen. He robbed his first bank at age thirty-five with two guys named Dan and Jack, a father-and-son team who were local electrical contractors. They were proficient in their trade, especially when it came to the security systems that they were often called to work on. One system, in particular, was the one protecting the Citizens Bank in a small town about forty-five miles from where they lived. George was very good with cutting tools and cutting torches and had access to both.

Dan's son Jack had been friends with George since their grammar school days. One night, while sitting on a porch, drinking beer and complaining about work, Dan said, "We should just rob a bank and quit working."

George thought Dan was shitting him. It turned out that Dan and Jack had been planning a caper for some time and were just waiting for the right moment to spring it on George.

"Why the hell not?" George said, knocking back another sip of beer. "Here's to making a big withdrawal."

Dan and Jack had already figured out how to disable the alarms of the bank they planned to rob. They decided to break in during a weekend, hoping to go in unnoticed. If they could not open the vault, they would steal from the safety-deposit boxes. The plan worked like a charm. They stashed the car a few blocks away in an abandoned garage and carried their gear to the bank. Dan tossed a rope with a grappling hook attached to it on to the roof, gave it a few tugs, and the rope went tight. With a rope ladder tied to his waist, he pulled himself up.

On the roof Dan tied off one end of the ladder to a vent stack and threw the other over the side. George and Jack climbed it while carrying most of the tools. Dan pulled the heavier gear up with a rope, hand over hand, with Jack helping him lift the bags over the roof's edge. Dan and Jack tore into the bags for measuring tapes and paint, then laid out the spot above the vault where George would cut through with an electric drill plugged into a wire that Jack had spliced from an outdoor light. George drilled holes three inches apart along the lines they had painted, looking for spots between the rebar that was embedded in the concrete.

George cut through the rebar with a torch as Dan and Jack covered the flame with a tarp. A concrete slab fell to the vault floor, where it smashed into pebbles and opened a space for Dan to drop a rope ladder. He climbed down into the darkness with two lamps over his shoulder. The job had gone so quickly, the three robbers had time to clean out the vault and open the safety-deposit boxes, too. Torching the boxes open might have damaged the loot. George knew that it was easier to just punch out the locks with a chisel and pry open the doors with a crowbar.

George was amazed at the shit people put in those things. One out of every three boxes was full of worthless crap that he just dumped out onto the floor. But the others were a smorgasbord of jewelry, diamonds, gold, cash, and bonds. The men were in there for so long that Dan sent Jack up and out through the rabbit hole in the roof and down the street to a deli for sandwiches and drinks. Jack paid for the meals with a pocket full of cash that he had liberated from a box numbered 109.

They cleared out as soon as they had taken everything worth taking. The only things they left behind were three big piles of shit, a big puddle of piss, and a few silk scarves with gold monograms discovered in one of the boxes, which they used to wipe their asses. They did two more jobs the same way in different cities over the next six months, including the calling cards.

The newspapers ran stories about the robberies, detailing how three individuals were emptying the vaults and safety-deposit boxes and leaving excrement behind. George and his fellow bandits thought leaving it was hilarious. Looking back on it, he realized that it didn't take a forensic specialist to figure out that the same three robbers were doing each and every job, in a manner of speaking.

The investigators interviewed victims and took inventories of the safety-deposit boxes. They put the word out to all the pawnbrokers and jewelry stores in three counties to be on the lookout for certain items. One day, Jack took a big old diamond ring into a jewelry store to get it appraised. The old guy behind the counter raised an eyebrow at him and told him to hold on a minute and he'd be right back just before he ducked into a back room. When it came to things like electrical work and bank robbery, Jack was pretty sharp. As for anything else, he was as smart as a bag of hammers.

As Jack waited for the old dude to come back, two cops came

through the front door. They walked straight up to Jack and asked him his name, which he told them. They asked him where he got the ring. He blurted out, "I found it!"

The cops smirked just before they spun him around and bent him over the glass showcase and slapped the handcuffs on him. They took the diamond ring from the old guy and said, "Let's take a little ride and talk about this ring you found, Jack."

Jack couldn't think on his feet as the questions were being fired off at him. When the FBI took over his interrogation, it was all over for him. When they asked him about the bank robberies, he broke down.

Jack didn't give up his partners, but it didn't take them long to figure out who he had been hanging around with for the last few months. The boys had been spending money like they had just won the sweepstakes. The cops pinned all the robberies on them, thanks to the piles of shit. George, Dan, and Jack were hardly professional fuckin' bank robbers. They were just three guys who hatched a plan one night drunk on beer, then went for it. That's how they all got thirty-eight years in prison.

Prison had been George's home ever since. His wife divorced him after the third year, but she still visited him and sent him stuff. George had been denied parole seven times. In about three weeks he would probably be denied again.

I couldn't help but think how similar the ending of George's bank-robbing career was to the end of my smuggling days. No matter how many guys are involved in the crime, it only takes one to bring the others down. George was a little unsettled after mentioning his ex-wife. He was expecting a visit from her the next day, and I was expecting a visit from my dad and mom. They were bringing my niece Tina to visit also. I hadn't seen her since she was born nearly four years earlier.

We ended our games for the night early so I could try to read myself to sleep. Damn visits always made me anxious.

The next morning the guys in my unit who were expecting visitors were busy showering and shaving and putting on their best prison khakis. I completed my shower and dress ritual early in the morning before the lights came on. I had always kept a little something special in my locker for just these occasions. Working in the library, I was privileged to be the first to go through the new magazines. When they arrived, I would remove all of the scratch-and-sniff ads for new colognes. These were great for just such events because, after all, who the fuck else am I going to smell good for in this place? The days of club hopping, dancing, and sleeping with Lori were gone. All I had to do to apply the scent was get the strip wet with a little water, then rub it on my neck, and, presto, cologne. The scratch-and-sniffs were a very popular item with cons, but I never charged them a dime for the scents. It was, in a way, a public-relations tool for me.

George and I were finally called, so we made our way into the strip-down area. All inmates going to and coming from visitation are subject to a strip search. You go into a little room, take off all your clothes, and while one guard searches through your clothing and shoes, another one conducts a visual search of your naked body. It goes something like this: raise your arms, open your mouth, stick out your tongue, lift your tongue, run your fingers through your hair and behind your ears, lift your nut sack, turn around, bend over, and spread your cheeks, lift each foot to show the underside, put your clothes back on, and go meet your visitor all strip-searched and clean.

When you finally do make it into the visitation room and catch up with your guests, the rules are simple. One kiss and one hug when you meet. If your visitor is a girlfriend or a wife, holding hands is permitted only in plain view of the guards watching your every move. You can either sit inside or outdoors in the broiling Florida sun. I always chose to sit inside to take advantage of the air-conditioning. When George and I had visits at the same time, we always sat together. He got to know some of my family and I got to know his ex-wife, Mary. Our visits lasted an hour, but they seemed like only five minutes. Visitation allowed me not only to share time with loved ones but also to relax. For a short time, I let my guard down and did not worry about always looking over my shoulder. My dad took it all in stride, but my mom had a bit of a time getting used to the idea of sitting in a room filled with criminals. My niece Tina was my brother Pat's firstborn, and she was totally immune to the fact that she was at a prison. She sat in the chair next to me for a brief moment, swinging her legs, sipping her soda, and crunching on her potato chips before she jumped up and ran around like any four-year-old. The typical questions regarding prison life came first from my dad. Because this was her first and, as it turned out, only visit, my mom tearfully asked how I had handled the past few years. After we caught up on all the life I had missed and after the tears were finished, I was permitted one more kiss and hug before heading back to that little room to be violated once again before returning home.

Back in the yard I often thought to myself that the visits did more good for the people visiting than they did for us cons. I wanted to just give up on seeing family and friends because it was too hard to reenter prison and leave the ones I loved behind. It was almost like reliving the first day I got there all over again. I spent a few hours wiping tears from my face while reacclimating to that fucking hole.

My days on the high seas, smuggling marijuana, making millions of dollars, living in exotic locales—those days seemed like a distant star to me as I lay there in my prison bunk. Those days were just stories that I used to entertain the other cons. And keep myself sane. Sometimes, I could almost see those ships out on the horizon, and I could almost smell that fragrant weed as it drifted on Gulf breezes. Was it all just a dream?

CHAPTER THIRTEEN

I remembered one particular ship, especially, that smelled like Caribbean potpourri and was commanded by a mélange of a crew. There was a dreadlocked Jamaican Rastafarian, a Frenchman with a crew cut from the north end of St. Martin, and a Dutch captain from the south end of St. Martin. And then there was Norman. Norman was a juvenile orangutan who had been won by the Frenchman in a poker game in Honduras during a six-day layover due to a storm off the north coast of Cuba. After a few days at sea they let the little fucker out to stretch his legs and then could not catch him as we unloaded the ship. Norman was a humanlike little critter with long flowing strands of red hair draping his back and arms like a cape, swinging above our heads from the antennas and the ship's rigging. While we unloaded the bales, the Dutch captain regaled us with the details of Norman's acquisition and his crew's reluctance to have him aboard any longer. Our arrival had only heightened the little guy's anxiety. He had been on that ship for five days, and when we pulled alongside, I guess the poor bastard thought that it was his opportunity to escape. He leaped from their wheelhouse roof to ours, only to discover that our boat was almost as confined as his home on the ship. We continued with the off-load as Norman screamed and leaped back and forth from ship to ship.

This job was remembered by anyone who had a hand in its off-loading. Not only was Norman on board, but so were fourteen tons of sweet-smelling Jamaican Lion's Herb, the nicest prize to come across our deck in a long time. The gleaming sticky buds had a devastating and inebriating aroma with a sweet and spicy taste. The packaging also set this load apart from all the rest. When I first climbed into the hold, I expected to see stacks of neatly pressed bundles. What I found were approximately six hundred neatly stacked boxes marked with a bold Marlboro logo. They were about thirty-six inches tall by twenty-four inches wide and nearly fourteen inches deep, and each was packed with twenty individually pressed and wrapped one-kilo bricks of tasty weed. My crew was surprised to discover how well the stuff was packaged but not surprised by the attempt at disguise the pot. I had seen similar loads like this one a few years back that used bags labeled "Purina Horse Chow." Only then did I realize that Purina produced more than just dog chow and puppy chow. The load was easy to move, and that made getting the bundles back to the house a breeze, which translated into an early night.

When we shoved off, the ship's captain pointed up at the top of our antenna and in his Dutch accent yelled out, "Hey dere! You boys go 'head and keep dat dere monkey!"

Clark, Captain Red, and I all turned at the same time and looked up, and there that little fucker was, hanging on to the antenna with both hands and both of his creepy handlike feet. That antenna was the receiving array for LORAN (Long-Range Aid to Navigation), which was the largest and stoutest antenna on the boat. It was as thick as a mast, nearly four inches at its base and rising fifteen feet above the wheelhouse roof, tapering off to a slender diameter of two inches. Our boat rolled from side to side on the evening swells, and so did the antenna, now burdened with the weight of that damn ape. Once again little Dutch boy shouted, "Yeah, dat's right! You boys over dere, I said, you just go 'head and keep dat fuckin' monkey, OK?!"

"Fuck no!" I yelled back. "There's no way we're taking that thing with us! What the hell are we gonna do with it?!"

Captain Red gunned the throttle, which startled Norman. His (Norman's, not Captain Red's) jungle senses took over. The boats pitched and danced. The antenna swayed toward the ship for barely a second, just long enough for Norman to let go. That little fucker stretched out his arms, and for a brief few seconds he appeared to hang in midair as he sailed across the expanse between our two vessels with his amber cape gently fluttering behind him. He flew to the other boat, landing creepy-feet first right on that captain's chest. Norman seemed to scream, as if to say, *You're not leaving me behind! You fucker!* Those feet had a death grip on the lapels of the man's jacket, and Norman's arms windmilled like a freestyle swimmer's as he proceeded to bitch-slap the shit out of that captain.

Red threw it in gear, punched the throttle, and we left that freak show in our wake. The weather wasn't bad. The wind started to pick up just a bit, but that was always a good thing. The rougher the weather, the better chance that we were the only ones out there.

The only house available was an old stilt home built close to the water's edge that had roughly nine hundred square feet of living area and was safely elevated about ten feet aboveground, in case of a storm surge. The house was loaded, and everyone was home safe by one a.m. That's about the time C. W. Saunders showed up on the island. C.W. was the sheriff and a force to be reckoned with in town. He wasn't a stupid man, he knew as well as anyone else what was going on, but he had to see it first before he could do anything about it. He was a friend to everyone and a handyman/jack-of-all-trades when he wasn't being the sheriff.

C.W. would lend a hand to anyone who needed it. He helped me move my trailer across the island one summer day after one of the guys decided to build a giant log-cabin-style home right where it had been sitting for years.

C.W. was out there that night snooping around for some reason. Apparently, some Yankee had been disturbed from his sleep by the noise of fast boats running without lights. Our lookout back at the stash house keyed his radio to say that C.W. had parked his patrol car just down the street from the house and was now watching it. He could only see the front from where he sat. The rest of the house was obscured by coconut palms, banana trees, and other island vegetation. The breeze had picked up, which worked in our favor because it kept the smell of marijuana out of C.W.'s face. But the wind was taking its toll on the now top-heavy stilted home we were using. The light-gray, sun-bleached two-by-sixes that we'd been stepping on were also warped and splitting at their ends. With each gust of wind, the nails that secured the boards to the treads were pulled up, ever so slightly. The fucking place was falling apart as it gently swayed from side to side whenever the wind picked up, and it strained under the weight of, for all intents and purposes, six hundred cases of Marlboro cigarettes.

Meanwhile, our guy Sambo, a twenty-year-old blond-haired, blue-eyed, barefoot crazy-ass son of a bitch who possessed the amount of education you could coax from the remaining two inches of a dull No. 2 pencil, sat in the bushes next to C.W.'s car. His job was to babysit him and sit close enough to hear the police radio. Somehow, it seemed fitting that Sambo had drawn babysitting duty because just a week earlier he had been ticketed by C.W. for driving while intoxicated—while he was on his lawnmower! The day he was cited, Sambo was on his riding lawnmower, headed to Clark and Kat's place for dinner, when C.W. came up behind him. An intense five-and-a-half-miles-per-hour pursuit ensued across the island as Sambo finished his last two beers before coming to a stop.

We had to unload the merchandise from the house without C.W. spotting us. We called about a dozen of the guys to bring their T-Crafts back over to Johnny's, then go back to the stash house and wait for their boats to arrive. To avoid being heard again and to avoid letting the smell of outboard engine exhaust waft across the island, Johnny and Todd strung all the boats together and used paddles to pull them along like pack mules. Coming from Johnny's, they rounded the back side of the island and eased them into position. With the boats now clustered around the dock just outside the house, the unloading commenced. The pot-packed house was so top-heavy on those stilts that simply walking up and down the stairs caused it to sway nearly out of control, so we passed the bundles like a bucket brigade down the stairs and into the waiting boats. The last guy to exit the house locked the door behind him, quietly descended the stairs, and jumped into one of the reloaded T-Crafts with the rest of us. By 4:40 a.m., we had paddled all six hundred bundles across the bay, up Turner River to our waiting Winnebago and a tractor trailer, and put it on the road to Miami. Then we all went home. All of us except Sambo. He waited there in the bushes next to C.W. until daybreak. Sambo woke up the sheriff with a gentle tap on the hood of his car as he passed and greeted him with a brisk "Good morning, Charlie!" Then he strolled across the street and disappeared behind the front door of his trailer and turned his porch light off.

CHAPTER FOURTEEN

In 1986, two years after the Feds tried to take down the Saltwater Cowboys, the jobs were still coming, fast as ever. We handled them all with ease—all, that is, except for one job in particular. At the time, though, the mission seemed to be by the book. Carlito and Leo had their ship bring the pot up from Colombia. All we had to do was meet it offshore, unload it, and deliver the haul to them somewhere in Miami. No problem.

The method of delivery was the same as always. The shore crew utilized all manner of transportation to deliver the bales to a strip mall, where our respective drivers would do their respective dances. You know the drill by now. The Cubans were cautious that way, and that was fine by me. But what they didn't comprehend was the loyalty among my crew members and how that trust was a big reason why we were all getting rich. In those days, if one of our guys got busted with a truck- or carload of pot, he was only going to get fourteen to eighteen months in a Club Fed. That's what we called a federal prison located on an air force base or any other type of military installation. The surroundings and daily routine of a Club Fed could be compared to those of summer camp. The rest of us would take care of the guy's family until he came home. Then he went right back to work again. So back to the story.

This was a dangerous two-night job. Dangerous because none of us really wanted to press our luck by approaching the same vessel twice. But in this case we had no choice. Sixty-two thousand pounds of weed were on board. I asked Jorge to bring to me a schematic of the ship so I could tell the guys how to load it. I took the drawings and examined the ship's holds and other watertight compartments below deck. Looking closely I noticed a maintenance bilge in the bow section beneath a dry storage area known as the folks hold. This bilge area was accessible through a watertight hatch in a maintenance compartment just aft to (or behind) the hold. I explained to Jorge that he needed to compress his bales no larger than the size of that hatch's opening because this was where we would store half of the load, 31,000 pounds. Those bales would be hidden in the bilge until the second night of work. If any problems arose or any delays occurred while the first half was on its way to Miami, the second half would be well concealed until we could reapproach the ship or send it to an alternate drop point. When closed, the top of the bilge hatch rose only four inches above the floor in the nine-foot-by-nine-foot enclosed maintenance compartment. Because all of the compartments on this type of vessel were fitted with watertight doors, the threshold through the doorway to this room rose twelve inches above the floor. So six inches of wet cement could then be poured over the floor to cover the hatch and conceal it from view. The added touches of a few buckets, mops and the random broom topped off with a few rags tossed around would easily turn the space into a storage room, or so it would appear. Meanwhile the other

31,000 pounds of weed would be stacked in the midship hold (the center hold in the ship) just below the weather deck.

We would bring in the 31,000 pounds the first night, then come back the second night for the balance. This would give the ship's crew time to jackhammer the concrete from atop the bilge hatch so we could get the last load out, and we would all go on our merry way.

Our boats loaded that first night with no problems until about three hours into our trek back to shore, when the mother ship called out to us over the radio. The captain was obviously in a panic as he described to us how a low-flying plane had just passed right over them. It was most likely the Coast Guard out of Fort Myers or Tampa. The captain kept hailing us over and over again, requesting the assistance of our chase boat. At that time there was no moon and the night sky was totally dark. Our luck held out and I concluded that we weren't spotted because no airplane had flown over us and there was nothing on the radar for twenty-five miles except the freighter.

I didn't respond to his call. To do so would have given us away. There simply wasn't anything we could do about it, and I wasn't about to give up our only lifeline. The chase boat was going to stay with us no matter what. Those guys on the ship knew the risks. Besides, I still wasn't sure if we had been spotted, too. My first priority was to put as much distance as possible between us and them. So we throttled up, pushing our engines to the breaking point, and cruised onward toward shore to get ourselves unloaded.

Back onshore with our first load stashed in a safe house, word was already circulating that a Coast Guard cutter had been dispatched to investigate our mother ship.

The next morning, as we sent off the first load to Miami, I learned that the Coast Guard and US Customs had in fact boarded and seized the mother ship. They were taking it to the Port of Tampa along with its crew. So much for the second half of the load. Or so we thought.

It was unfortunate that the crew was taken into custody, but like I said, that's the risk we all take. The ship was searched from top to bottom. Fortunately for my crew it was not searched very well. As it turned out, the residue left behind from the bales we took out of the midship hold led the Feds to believe that they had been denied their prize. They believed that we had gotten away with the entire load. The residue also masked any scent of the 31,000 pounds that were still hidden in the bilge beneath six inches of concrete, and as a result, the second half of the load was never discovered. This is where the story takes a wild turn.

You see, we never allowed the owners of those ships to actually captain them or the owners of the vehicles to actually drive them. That would be plain silly. What our captains and drivers were instructed to do upon being boarded or stopped was simply radio back to home base and let us know that the end was inevitable. Then the owners would be contacted to immediately report their vessels or vehicles as having been hijacked or stolen, which would relieve them of any responsibility for its involvement in unlawful activities. Therefore, because the ship was of Panamanian registry and because there was no further need of the ship as evidence—because we had gotten away with the entire load (wink, wink)—three months later the vessel was deported back to Panama and into the hands of its rightful owner. The reported hijacking and subsequent deportation of the vessel was standard operating procedure, so with the help of the Panamanian government, in this case General Manuel Noriega, the owner put another crew on the ship and sent it back to us.

We met the vessel one more time, and the crew jackhammered that bilge hatch open; then we proceeded to haul the last of the ship's bounty to shore.

Those clowns in Tampa never knew what was right under their noses. None of us could believe that we had just pulled off the impossible. One week later during the money count for this job, there came a personal message from General Noriega and a bonus. The message simply said, in Spanish, "Unbelievable! Thank you, my friend." And the bonus was an extra $5 a pound on top of the $165 I originally had charged him—higher than usual because of our double exposure to the ship.

CHAPTER FIFTEEN

The Saltwater Cowboys were in demand. That same summer of 1986, I agreed to do another job for my friends from Miami. This time we would bring in fifteen tons. The vessel would come closer to shore and anchor about twenty miles southwest of a small outer island called Pavilion Key. This key is located on the northwest corner of our Ten Thousand Islands and is near the Everglades National Park border. The load would arrive by way of a stripped-out sixty-foot yacht. These yachts were used frequently for two reasons: first of all, it wasn't uncommon for a vessel of that type to be in this particular area, and second, a boat this size could easily store the fifteen tons of tightly packed bales below deck and out of sight.

I liked those types of jobs for the simple reason that the closer we could get the boats to shore, the faster we could get them unloaded and stashed. In this case I would guide the boat to shore from forty miles out, and then the smaller, faster boats could take the bales directly to the stash house. By doing this I eliminated the need for a crab boat to go offshore and bring the load to us. From a business point of view it meant that since I didn't have to pay that extra boat or boats, my share of the take would increase by the amount saved. Meanwhile, the price for intercepting the load and taking it to Miami remained the same. It didn't matter if I used ten thousand fuckin' pelicans to do the job; they still had to pay me $145 for every pound.

The way this job was set up was no different from the way I had done it a hundred times before. I could communicate with the load boat by way of a powerful single sideband radio. Single sideband allowed me to communicate with our boat even as it was sitting just off the coast of Barranquilla in Colombia. It allowed us to relay any needs or concerns to each other regarding fuel, food, water, or medical supplies. More important, I could let them know if this area was being too heavily patrolled, requiring them to delay their arrival. The radio was also used to let me know of their progress, specifically if they would be on time.

Everything had gone as planned. The ship had no real problems. It was smooth sailing—so smooth, in fact, the vessel had made better time than I had expected. My entire crew would be ready to work. They were to be straight and sober, fueled up and ready to go on the night the job was to be done. What they did before then, I could give a shit. But when the time came, they all needed to have their shit together because if they screwed it up, they would never work with me or anyone else again and they all knew this. One thing was for sure, when they were sober, I trusted each and every one of them to do their part, and they trusted me. They also knew that if one of them screwed up it could cost us all our freedom or at the least millions of dollars. So they all took this work pretty seriously. Even though we all knew exactly what to do, we never relaxed our guard. Our intelligence was gathered on every front. Local sheriffs, local marine patrol, Coast Guard, and highway patrol were all under surveillance. We knew where everybody was from the time the load boat was emptied to the time the shit got to Miami the next day. As I said earlier, this job had gone very well so far.

The day before the load was scheduled to arrive, I received a call from the captain. He was calm and matter-of-fact, so I knew he wasn't having any problems. We talked a little bit about the weather and the conditions of the seas. It was typical radio chat between two seamen until he mentioned the fact that everything had gone so well he would be on the hill tonight. That meant he would be on the spot one night earlier than planned. I immediately cut in.

"I didn't expect you for another day, and it's not possible to unload your catch until then," I said. "There is no way I can pull my guys together at a moment's notice. Most of them are out partying."

Then he came back on the radio in a panic.

"You need to come and get us off this shit, or I'm dumpin' it!" he cried. "Do you hear me? I'm dumpin' it!"

I wasn't prepared for his ultimatum. He was now royally pissin' me off, and I let him have it.

"Listen to me, you fuckin' moron. If you had bothered to take your head out of your ass long enough to let me know your status, I would have been ready for you!"

But this asshole was freakin' out and couldn't be reasoned with. It was probably his first haul.

"Keep your shit together and shut the fuck up!" I hollered over the radio. "I'll get to you somehow, you fuckin' pussy!" Then for good measure I added, "Just so you know . . . if you guys throw that catch overboard for no good reason . . . Leo will probably shoot you with that fuckin' gun he keeps tucked in his belt!"

I was too fucking pissed at the time to realize just how dangerous this conversation was becoming. I slammed the mic down on the kitchen table, ran to the door, and jumped into my Corvette and left Chokoloskee doing a hundred miles an hour across the causeway into Everglades City. I was hoping to find my old friend Gary.

Gary operated his own private air tours of Everglades National Park and the Ten Thousand Islands. The hundreds of waterways keep park rangers busy all year long with search-and-rescues of visitors who get turned around and lose their way, but seen from above, the beautiful and lush tropical forests come alive. Nowhere is the scope of this labyrinth built by Mother Nature better appreciated than by air. But I wasn't going sightseeing.

Gary could usually be found at the Captains Table, a local resort hotel with a restaurant, bar, and pool. Besides being a tour pilot, he was also the manager of the hotel, which for him was a great combination. I parked my Corvette in the hotel parking lot, then made my way to the office door as I had done many times before. Through the window I could see the top of his head behind the front desk. His personality and his job were a perfect marriage. He was as jolly and witty as he was energetic. His hair was just beginning to show a hint of gray, which was all I could see of his five feet, six inches from this vantage point. Behind him on the wall was a giant sign that read "Happy Gary's Airplane Tours." When I walked into his office, he leaped up from his chair with a smile and greeted me with a handshake. His energy sparked when I told him that I needed him to take me up immediately. Then, I handed him $500 and explained that I meant right fucking now. Although my business was never discussed with him in any way, he was no dummy. He knew as well as a lot of the other locals just what that business involved, though nobody spoke about anyone or to anyone about anything.

We drove in separate cars to the small Everglades City airstrip and boarded his single-engine Cessna. Five minutes later we were airborne and Gary asked, "Where are we goin'?"

I spoke up over the roar of the engine.

"We're goin' offshore, Gary. Take a heading of two hundred and seventy-five degrees."

That was all I said, nothing else. Thirty minutes into the flight I spotted the yacht. It was important for me to see for myself the exact location of the boat and circle it to be sure no other vessels were in sight of it. Then we flew back to Everglades City.

Once we got back on the ground, I went straight to pick up Todd, one of my badass crewmen from the Jersey Shore and the older brother of my pal Scotty "Bam Bam" Bigelow. Then we went to a private dock where we kept one of our chase boats. This one was mine, the Chris-Craft Scorpion, which had a deep V-hull and was built for speed and rough seas.

It was four o'clock in the afternoon as we made our way out through the pass. Cruising at a comfortable fifty-five miles per hour, we reached the yacht and its freaked-out captain and two crew members in about an hour. The sun had just begun to set when Todd and I pulled alongside, gathered them up in our craft, and left the boat at anchor with its cargo. We would return the next night as originally planned to bring it inshore for the off-loading.

On our way back to shore I got in that captain's face. I tore him a new asshole again for waiting until the last minute to tell me he was coming in early. Even though he was working for my Miami friends, reaming him was still my job. After all, my crew and I were the ones handling that shit and putting our lives at risk. Todd had been silent the whole time I chewed this guy out.

"Why don't you let me throw this motherfucker overboard, Tim?" Todd chimed in.

His suggestion was very appealing to me, but I didn't give it serious consideration. Todd kept looking right into the frightened captain's eyes.

"We can pick him up tomorrow when we come back. That is, if he's still treadin' water."

"No, let it go, Todd," I said. Now, I was looking the captain in the eye. "I'm sure Leo will take care of this prick."

I told the boys in Miami that I didn't know where they found this fool but that I would never work with him again. What we had to do was far too risky—first off, leaving the boat at anchor with nobody onboard and, second, having to approach it twice.

The following afternoon, which was the day the job was originally scheduled to go down, everyone was sober and ready to work. I timed our approach to the load boat to be just after sundown. As we got closer to the sixty-foot yacht, Todd noticed a light was on in the wheelhouse.

"Did you leave that goddamn light on?" I screamed at Captain Chickenshit.

He shrugged.

"Maybe I did. After all, it was still light out when you guys got to us."

Not thinking much more about it, I continued cruising toward the boat. We made our approach, and just as we were getting prepared to throw our lines up to tie off, we heard someone yell from the rail above:

"This is the United States Customs. Stand fast! Put your hands on your head!"

Well, that wasn't going to happen.

"Fuck you!" I shouted into the darkness. "I don't think so!"

Then I pushed my throttles full forward and took off like a bat out of hell. With my heart and mind racing, I looked back to see if they were in pursuit, but all I saw were muzzle flashes. These assholes were shooting at my engines! With my throttles wide open, we tore through the water doing seventy miles per hour before anyone's ass could hit the seat. Running east toward land, I was trying to get into the safety of the islands before anyone caught up with us. I turned to Captain Fuckup with fire in my eyes.

"I should've let Todd throw your ass off the boat yesterday," I yelled over the roar of my engines. "If I didn't think you'd rat us out, I'd throw you off right fuckin' now!"

This was not the first time Todd and I had been chased by the Feds. A few years earlier we had been chased by US Customs' new offshore interdiction vessel. They called it *Blue Thunder*, and they were very proud of that big bastard. But the only thunder it made was when we ran it aground. A big offshore boat like that one wasn't designed to run in the shallow backwaters, but our boats were. The Cape Romano area of the Ten Thousand Islands is notorious for its sandy bottom that shifts quite frequently during any type of storm event. Todd and I had investigated this area's bottom the day before in order to discover the exact location of the deepwater passage leading to the back side of the cape. So we used this bit of drafting to our advantage when *Blue Thunder* came after us. We had just finished unloading one quiet evening at Cape Romano, south of Marco Island. The smaller boats had all made it to the stash house just to the north of us inside Caxambas Pass when we heard it. It wasn't like it was going to sneak up on us because you could hear that fucker's motors roaring when it left Fort Myers Beach, and that was ten miles away! It was my job to distract customs, so the trick was to draw them into shallow water through a false pass by trimming our motors vertically and horizontally to lessen our draft. We allowed that big bastard to follow us as closely as we felt comfortable into the shallows. Then, just when they thought they were about to overtake us, we heard the sound of thunder, all right. It was the sound of that big piece-of-shit's engines going wild as it slid up onto the sandbar we had just skipped. *Blue Thunder* came to an abrupt stop. While the crew walked around their boat, wondering what the hell had just happened, we sat in the deepwater passage that they couldn't reach, smokin' a fat one, laughin' our asses off. With bandannas covering our faces, we headed out of the pass and south toward home, leaving our terrible nemesis behind us, a castaway in the darkness.

There Todd and I were again, being chased on the open water by US Customs. Yet in this case, I guess we were just too fast for them or they had expected us to just give up because no one chased us—or if they did, they were so far behind that we couldn't see them.

There are always lessons to be learned, even in our business. Hindsight being twenty-twenty, I should have circled that damn yacht first. But that lesson is left for another time; this time we had gotten away with our asses intact. We lost the load, but that was just a part of this dangerous game we played.

Over the next several days the people of Everglades City and Naples buzzed like bees with the news of a captured vessel loaded with marijuana. It made the front page of the local newspaper. The story said that the smugglers were not apprehended, but the investigation would continue. By this time we were all safe at home. I read the story back at my place, and I asked my pal Todd a rhetorical question:

"What are they possibly investigating? They got the boat, but they didn't get us."

Todd said, "Hell . . . they didn't even see who we were! We had bandannas over our faces. All they saw of us was our asses as we were pulling away from them!"

I could only laugh.

"Sometimes you catch the shark, and sometimes the shark catches you," I said. "It just wasn't this shark's day."

I tossed Johnny the comics section and turned on the TV just in time to catch the end of a Road Runner cartoon. The Road Runner left Wile E. Coyote standing motionless before a cloud of dust that stretched to the horizon. I couldn't help but laugh out loud. I was the fucking Road Runner! *MEEP! MEEP!*

At Chokoloskee Bay, 1986.

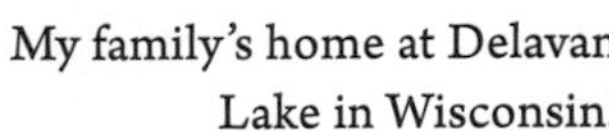

My family's home at Delavan Lake in Wisconsin.

My view of Delavan Lake from my family's home.

Clark and me aboard the *Difficult Days*, the first boat we worked on with Captain Red.

Lori and me at a nightclub in 1985.

The famous lobster roundabout in Nassau, Bahamas.

Moose and me at home on Paradise Island, Bahamas.

Having a good time at home after the casino.

Moose's burial at sea after a crazy night in the Bahamas.

The Mustang Clark and I drove from Wisconsin to Florida to find our new lives.

My high school graduation in 1976.

y first chase boat, the *Pair A Dice.*

A postcard I sent my parents from Chokoloskee Island. I wrote that "I live in a really nice trailer . . . for 35 bucks a month. I am working as a carpenter for $5.00/hour cash 7 days a week."

Naples Daily News

...th Year — No. 78 | Six sections — 74 Pages | WEDNESDAY AFTERNOON, OCTOBER 19, 1988 | 35 cents a copy

...aples puts brakes on 5th Avenue one-way plan until May

...LORI DARVAS

...City Council, in an unexpected vote today, decided ...delay a one-way street experiment in Naples Fifth ...enue South shopping district until May 1.

...ast week, council members endorsed making a ...-block section of Fifth Avenue one way westbound from U.S. 41 to Eighth Street. They said the change should ease congestion at U.S. 41 and Fifth Avenue South by eliminating eastbound traffic at the busy intersection.

The change, called an experiment, was to begin the weekend of Nov. 19-20 and run through the winter tourist season.

But today, Mayor Edwin Putzell began the regular City Council meeting by reading a three paragraph statement noting concerns of business owners and proposing a delay in the experiment until after the tourist season. Council members agreed. The one-way street issue was not on today's agenda.

The decision was a victory for merchants concerned that the one-way street would confuse customers, inviting them to shop elsewhere during the busy Christmas and tourist seasons.

More than 100 shop owners and employees in the area signed a petition of protest urging a delay in the experiment, said Carrie Burkhardt, co-president of the Fifth Avenue Merchants Association.

She added that merchants were happy with today's decision and look forward to working with city officials to solve traffic congestion and parking problems in the business district.

...Area part of U.S. pot dragnet

Agents say 38 helped import over 150 tons

By BRENNA KRIVISKEY
Staff Writer

Federal and local authorities today arrested 38 people who allegedly conspired to bring about 300,000 pounds of marijuana into Southwest Florida last year.

- Related photo, 2A
- Another drug bust shuts Lee bar, 1B

At least five people in the Naples area were arrested in the operation, which netted suspects from across the United States.

Most of the marijuana, which had a street value of about $147 million, was seized last year in Collier and Lee counties, according to Larry Giliotti, chief of the Drug Enforcement Administration Task Force in Naples.

The following Naples area residents were arrested:

- Carlos Bolana
- Timothy McBride
- [illegible]
- Warren Stewart
- [illegible]

Most details of "Operation Peacemaker" were unavailable at presstime. A complete list of defendants and additional information on the case was to be presented at a 1 p.m. news conference in Fort Myers today.

The 38, who were arrested between 4 and 6 a.m. face federal charges of importation of marijuana and conspiracy to import and distribute marijuana in the United States.

They are scheduled to appear in federal court in Fort Myers sometime this afternoon.

The arrests stem from the second phase of "Operation Peacemaker," an investigation by several authorities into marijuana smuggling in Southwest Florida, Giliotti said.

More arrests are pending, Giliotti said.

...Sheriff's Office, the DEA, U.S. Customs, the State Attorney's Office, the Florida Department of Law Enforcement, the Florida Marine Patrol and the U.S. Marshal's Service participated in the operation.

Authorities made 12 arrests in Everglades City, more than in any other single location, Giliotti said.

In an effort to keep defendants from leaving the area, sheriff's deputies at about 3:45 a.m. blocked the way from Everglades City to U.S. 41 and asked travelers for identification.

Residents were cooperative and no one was arrested at the roadblock, officers said.

After the roadblock was in place, teams of officers sped through the dark streets of Everglades City in unmarked cars. They pulled up to the house of several suspects, ran out of their cars and yelled "Police, open up."

The lights went on not only in the house, but in the houses of curious neighbors.

Suspect Michael Parton, left, of Everglades C...

Jerry Foerman, arrested and en route to a police vehicle early today in his Everglades City front yard.

The front page of the *Naples Daily News,* October 19, 1988.

In federal prison in 1989. I was sentenced to ten years.

Graduating from my bank-robbing pal Dennis Lehman's fiction-writing class in prison.

Learning to swim in the tub. From left, me, Pat, and Mike.

My brother Pat going out for his first scuba dive.

The observation tower as seen from the Chokoloskee causeway.

Ernest Hamilton's iconic legacy was erected in the summer of 1984.

The concrete cap for the tower's left rear anchor and guy wire.

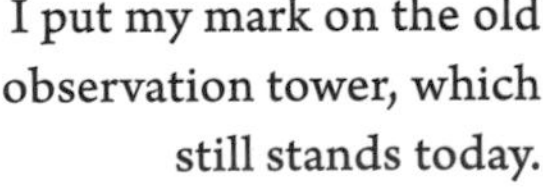

I put my mark on the old observation tower, which still stands today.

CHAPTER SIXTEEN

Prison is all about routine. Wake up, line up for meals, exercise, work my prison job, play cards with George, turn out the lights, go to sleep, and repeat the same thing every day for the next ten years.

One morning, I woke up at six a.m. to another day of routine. I had breakfast, then headed out to the weight pile and met Rolly to begin our daily three-and-a-half-hour workout. We were into the winter months, so I wasn't scheduled to work until this evening. During the day there weren't very many cons out in the yard because ninety percent of them were working, so after a hard workout, Rolly and I would usually play racquetball for a couple of hours or just sit out in the sunshine and soak up the warmth, watch each other's back, and read.

Reading was something I had never really done in my past life. But in prison it was a great way to pass the time and to believe I was somewhere else. Through reading, I could always transport myself faraway to another country and meet new people. I could climb a mountain or just be someone else on an adventure for a while. By that time I had read more than four hundred books, and I was getting pretty good at escaping that place in my mind.

The afternoon came and went, and it was once again time to head back inside to get locked down and be counted. The evening was one that I will never forget for the rest of my life. It's the evening that I almost got killed. As I'm sure I said before, prison is a very volatile place, and this evening the volatility was high.

Our unit had passed inspection, so we were let out first for chow. Breakfast, lunch, and dinner were all served cafeteria style. You grabbed a tray and proceeded down the line, and the guys working kitchen detail slapped your dinner on it. From there you made your way out into the dining room, where there was an island set up for you to choose your drink and your condiments. At that point, things could become a little bit tricky. Guys push and crowd in on one another like hogs to a trough. In prison, the only cons who respected one another were the ones who had been down for a while. The new fish, as we called the new arrivals, had not learned that. In this fucked-up place there were convicts, there were inmates, and there were jitterbugs, or "jitts" for short.

Convicts mind their own business. They know when to show respect, and that respect is returned. Inmates don't have respect for themselves. They snitch, and they make everybody's business their own. And then there are the jitterbugs. These fuckers are the young new breed of punks who have no respect for cons or inmates.

That particular day, the new fish who weren't yet assigned to a unit were released for chow the same time we were. As I backed away from the beverage island with my drink, I ran into a jitt. I turned and saw a young black kid, no taller than about five foot three, wearing part of his meal on his shirt, with some on his shoes and the rest on the floor. He looked up at me and said, "You motherfucker. Watch what the hell you're doin'!"

I was not going to take that shit.

"You can eat shit now, you little dick smoker," I fired back. Then I started to raise my voice: "If you weren't standin' in the crack of my ass, you wouldn't be wearin' your fuckin' dinner right now."

Then I laughed at him, which apparently pissed the little fucker off even more. He reminded me of a tiny ankle-biting dog that wouldn't shut up.

"I'll get you, you motherfucker," he sputtered. "I'll kill you!"

I rolled my eyes.

"You know where I live, ass wipe. It ain't like I'm goin' anywhere."

I walked toward my table, sat down, and enjoyed my dinner. I didn't give that little shit another thought. Then a guard who had watched the whole thing went over to the prick and told him, "Get the fuck out of my chow hall."

If you were there for years, there was a good chance that most of the guards had been there with you as well. Even though none of us trusted a guard any further than we could throw his ass, we all could agree when a new fish was out of line.

After chow, I returned to my unit, changed into my work clothes, and got ready to begin my evening at the library. All I can remember from that moment was that I was sitting at a concrete table, waiting to be counted, and I heard the sound of shoes running over the small stones that covered the ground. Then it happened . . . *BANG!* I was hit from behind on the side of the head with something hard. Next, I was getting my ass beat. My survival instincts took over, and I desperately tried to stand up to defend myself. But that was a little easier said than done. The table and bench I was sitting at had been bolted to the ground. I tried to maneuver myself around to get my legs out from under it in order to stand up. Three guys threw fists at every part of my head and body. At the same time, each of them continuously struck me with something that felt like hammers. I was in a struggle for my life. When I was finally able to stand up and turn around to defend myself, all I saw were their chickenshit asses running through the compound away from me. It took me a minute or so to get my shit together. Somebody came up next to me.

"Hey, buddy, you're bleeding like a stuck pig."

Blood dripped off my head down on to my left shoulder.

"Man, your ear is really fucked up."

I reached up and touched my ear, but I couldn't feel anything. It didn't even hurt. I must have been in shock. Rolly came running over, took off his shirt, and handed it to me.

"Here, Timmy, take this and cover that shit and go get yourself cleaned up," he said. "Put on a new shirt and get your ass back here before you miss the count and the guards find out what just happened."

I took his shirt, held it to the side of my head, and let it drape over my shoulder to cover up the blood. Then went back to my unit to assess my condition and execute a bit of damage control.

When I got there, I looked at my ear in the mirror. The force of the first blow to my head had split my ear in two, and that bitch just wouldn't stop bleeding. I did the best I could to clean it up and slow the bleeding, but that's all I could do. I flushed my bloody shirt and Rolly's down the toilet so the guards wouldn't find them, and I put on a new one. I pressed a handful of paper towels against the side of my head and made my way back just in time to get in line for work. The battle wound was on my left ear, which the guard did not see because he was on the right as I walked past him. I headed down the walk into the building, then sat behind my desk and kept out of sight of the guards.

I started to feel the reverberations of those blows from head to toe. My ears were ringing, and the pain was becoming almost unendurable. Dennis and Rolly helped me to try to get the bleeding stopped, but they couldn't stop the blood. It wasn't flowing like before, but it was still dripping. It was a long evening of trying to keep out of sight of the guards. I knew if they saw my wound there would be no doubt in their mind that a fight of some sort had taken place, and that would be enough reason for them to take me to the hole. I told myself there was no way in hell I was going to that fucked-up place if I could help it.

So with a little help from my friends, I managed to make it through the evening without a brush with the guards, then returned to my unit.

While locked in and waiting for ten o'clock count, I felt it was in my best interest to hide out in the dark shadows of the TV room and stay away from the guards. But my plan was short-lived. No sooner had I gotten settled in than a guard opened the door and shouted: "McBride, are you in here?!"

I looked up at him from the dark shadow I was hiding in and answered.

"Yeah, I'm here, boss."

He looked in the direction of my voice and with squinted eyes began moving his head back and forth, trying to spot me in the darkness.

"Come here, boy!"

As I approached him, he reached out and took me by the jaw. He then turned my head and looked at my ear.

"Yep, you're the guy I'm looking for."

He took me by the arm and walked me to the unit's main door, unlocked it and pushed me through. Once we were outside, the prick handcuffed my hands behind my back.

"Let's take a little walk. The captain would like to see you."

We began walking across the compound toward the captain's office, and Mr. Brown, the guard who was escorting me, began a prison yard interrogation of his own.

"Why don't you tell me how your ear got that way?"

Without looking at him I said, "Boss, I got hit from behind right over there at those tables while I was waiting to go to work tonight."

He leaned over next to my good ear and in a hushed voice said, "So tell me who hit ya."

Well, this asshole ought to know that there was no way in hell he was going to get me to tell him. He had been around long enough to know that the most important rule of the convict code is that no matter what goes on, *you don't rat!* Sure, I had just been cracked upside the head, beat on, and nearly killed, but that was my business and not his or the captain's. The matter would be taken care of my way, the prison way. A dozen or more of my old crew were there. The Bureau of Prisons policy was to try to assign inmates to facilities that were as close to their families as possible. Being that there were more than two hundred of us from the Everglades and surrounding area, and with only a handful of federal institutions within or even near the state of Florida, it was inevitable that some of us would wind up together. Plus, I had made new friends on the inside. We would get the bastards who did this to me.

"I got hit from behind, boss. I didn't see who did it."

"Are you sure that's the story you want to tell the captain?"

"It sure is, boss," I said with conviction, "because it's the only one I've got."

When I walked into the captain's office, I noticed right away that he had at least eight photographs of different cons lying on his desk facing my direction. I also noticed that among those eight photographs were the three jitterbugs who had jumped me. He knew who had jumped me. He just needed someone to confirm it.

"Do you recognize any of these guys?" the captain asked.

Standing there handcuffed and bleeding again on my shirt, I was certain he was fucking with me because all three of those little motherfuckers were in his bullshit photographic lineup. I wasn't going to play his game.

"Yeah, sure, that's Joe and that's Frankie," I said. "I see those guys every day. Joey's from E-unit. He works in the kitchen, and Frankie sucks dick for commissary and smokes over in C-unit."

"C'mon, smart-ass, point out the guys who jumped you!"

I pretended to study the pictures. I knew that some rat bastard had already given me up, and so did the fucking captain because he had just said "guys." I looked at him and again at Mr. Brown.

"I'm sorry, boss. I keep tellin' ya, I got jumped from behind and I didn't see who did this."

As the captain exhaled, his voice went from a high pitch to a low pitch.

"OK, walk across the hall to the physician's office and get that mess fixed up."

It took ten stitches to put my ear back together. Dr. Betsy Fucking Ross gave me two six-hundred-milligram tablets of Motrin to quiet the pounding in my head and told me, "If the bastard that did this to you had been just one inch farther round the side of your head, he would have struck you in the temple and killed your ass."

I later learned that each of the punks had slipped his Master Lock from his locker into a sock. The little shit who I backed into at dinner had come running up behind me with his two pals, swinging their locks over their heads. The first shot hit my ear, but the other blows, the body shots, were showing up all over me in the form of black and purple bruises. I was beginning to look like a fucking Dalmatian!

After I was all patched up, Mr. Brown took me back into the captain's office and stood me in front of his desk. Here we go again! This time the pictures were all different except for the three who'd clocked me.

"I'm going to ask you one more time," the captain said, "to show me the guys who did this to ya!"

I wasn't about to give them up. He knew that.

"I have no choice but to lock you up in the hole until our investigation into this matter is completed," he said.

So off to the hole I went.

Walking through the doors of the administrative segregation unit, Ad-Seg for short, I could feel the blast of cool air. Yes, air-conditioning. Where I lived, in A-unit, there was no air-conditioning, just a couple of big fans keeping the stale hot air circulating. But air-conditioning added no real comfort to where I was going. This was jail inside prison.

I was told by the guard to strip down bare-ass naked, then to put on a bright orange jumpsuit. Then came the handcuffs, belly chain, and leg shackles. Walking down the hall to my cell, we passed a table piled with paperbacks and I was permitted to grab about a dozen novels to read during my stay. I didn't know how long I was going to be there, but I knew what to expect: a one-man concrete cell with a stainless steel sink-and-shitter combination and a steel bunk secured to the block wall. The cell was furnished with a two-inch-thick mattress and a matching pillow, which added another two inches of comfort. The air would be so cold you could hang meat. I carried my linens with me, one towel and one sheet. I said that I knew what to expect because I had been locked down like this before during my transfer to this prison. That's why I grabbed the books.

My first prison experience in the hole was during my transfer from county jail. I was driven by van from Fort Myers, accompanied by two US Marshals to Metropolitan Correctional Center in Miami to await transfer to Tallahassee. When I arrived, I was taken to the hole and locked down. New inmates entering a facility must first be screened to make sure that their crime doesn't warrant segregation from the general population. I was in the hole with another guy, a Greek dude by the name of Nick Adopilous. He had already been there for two days and was about to be released into the general population. He and I got along great right off the bat. He had also already had time to get this cell figured out. Most jails keep the temperature in their cell blocks at ridiculously low levels to add to the overall discomfort that we're already experiencing. Nick had discovered that the vents were double-louvered, and it was possible to slide a perfectly shaped newspaper or magazine page between them and use the sheet to regulate the AC. It got rather comfortable at that point, and the next thing I knew he was gone. I held the cell alone for two days until I entered the prison's general population. The first bunk assignment I was given landed me right next to the TV. The damn thing was annoying—it was loud, and it was on all day. This sure as hell wasn't going to work, so I approached the guard handing out these assignments and respectfully requested to be moved. With a wave of his hand he said, "Just go find an empty bunk. Then come back and let me know where you are located and I'll move your card in the bed book."

We were living in what was known as the "glass house." There were two levels, and all of the exterior walls were lined with huge windows. And outside in the yard were trees and a lake with a walking path circling it. There were peacocks strutting around among the inmates, and I was told that those fuckers went into fits of screaming if you crossed into their territory. They made a perfect perimeter alarm, and when you couple that with the fact that the prison was just a stone's throw from the Miami zoo, you sure as hell weren't going anywhere without being heard.

Everywhere you stood, or if you were lying down in your bunk on the floor level, you had a clear view to an upper level that was nothing more than a huge balcony circling the entire building. That looked appealing to me, so I immediately ascended to that level. I crested the top of the stairs and walked forward, passing the restrooms. A few feet beyond a bank of telephones, the wall made an abrupt left turn, and there began the rows of cubicles, four bunks in each, that lined the giant glass windowed wall behind them. As I turned my head to glance into the first cubicle, I heard Nick's voice shout, "Hey, Timmy!" He was sitting on the right-side bottom bunk next to another fellow, and on the opposite bottom bunk sat an old man with a blanket wrapped around him, freezing his nuts off. I told my new friend Nick that I was looking for a new spot to crash, and he pointed to the bunk above the old man's head and said, "There's your new spot, Timmy!" I tossed my shit onto the bunk, then went and reported my new bed assignment to the guard. When I returned to get myself settled in, the old man was sitting there, rocking back and forth and saying, "Damn, itsa cold in thisa mothera-fuckera!" There was no mistaking the guy's Italian accent. Without saying a word, I climbed up onto my bunk and with a section of newspaper reached over and shut that fucking air right off. After climbing back down, I took a seat next to the old guy, and in minutes he began to warm up and dropped the blanket. Turning his head and shoulders like old guys do, he looked me in the eye and said, "You a smarta guy, Timmy. Tomorrow I'm a tella you whata we're gonna do. We're gonna get up, take a nicea walka over to the chowa halla, and we gonna get a nicea cup of coffee and a doughnut. Thena we gonna take a little walk around the lakea."

The entire time I sat next to this guy, a number of cons had walked by giving their respect and acknowledging him by calling out the name Sal. Some would address him as Papa Sal. When he headed to the can to take a piss, I asked Nick, "Who the fuck is this guy?" And he said, "Oh, that's Papa Sal, Salvatore Gambino—he was my partner on the outside." Turns out he and Papa Sal were busted in Fort Lauderdale with a little over 2,100 pounds of coke and were each handed down a mandatory twenty-five-year sentence. The old man took an interest in me for some strange reason while walking around the lake that day. I'm guessing that when he had discovered that I was doing a ten-year bit, he became curious as to how I was able to conduct myself as if I hadn't a care in the world, and that endeared me to him. Enough so that he asked me if I would have a talk with his nephew, who was involved in the same deal gone bad and had received the same sentence. He confessed to me that his nephew was about my age and wasn't handling it too well. I told him that for sure I would talk to him, but that it wasn't going to change the fact that it was his time to do and only he could learn how to do it. When I left MCC and Miami on a "con air" flight out of Homestead Air Force Base to my next home a few weeks later, I of course never saw either of them again.

Back to my stay in the hole in Tallahassee. I spent the next nine days eating, sleeping, reading, and freezing my ass off. I was permitted to have one shower during my stay.

The guard banged on the steel door of my cell one morning, yelling, "Strip down. It's shower time!"

I walked butt-ass naked over to the cell door, turned around with my hands behind my back, and stuck them through a small opening. The guard then put handcuffs on my wrists and instructed me to step away from the door and put my face against the wall.

When you're in the hole, you are never allowed out of your cell unless you're restrained. Stepping out, I saw two guards. One grabbed me by the arm and held on while the other guard placed shackles on my ankles. They walked me to the shower.

The shower was just a steel cage out in the open where a male—or female—guard stood watching my every move. The cage door was opened for me, and I stepped in; then they locked it behind me.

The same procedure they had used to put the handcuffs and shackles on me was now performed to take them off through a small opening in the cage door. I had five minutes to soap up, rinse off, and dry myself. Then I stuck my hands back through the doors, was chained and taken back to my cell, where a fresh jumpsuit awaited me.

I found it very hard to keep my mind in this place. When you're left alone twenty-four hours a day, your own thoughts can be a very dangerous thing. Without any other distractions it's hard to keep your mind from wandering outside those fences. You begin torturing yourself with thoughts of simple things like driving a car, taking a walk around your neighborhood, or just picking up the telephone and calling a friend. It's amazing when you think about just how much we take for granted in our everyday lives. It's impossible for the average person to understand this and cherish these things. It's terrible to think that a person has to be locked up like an animal and have all these simple pleasures stripped away before he comes to realize just how important they really are.

As I sat in that solitary cell, I came to realize that this puzzle that was my life would never be complete without those missing pieces. Thank God I grabbed those books.

On the ninth day of my stay, at about three o'clock in the afternoon, I got a visit from the captain. He tapped on my cell door, and through the little round viewing window I could see his finger motioning me to come to the door.

"How are you, Timmy? How is that ear doing?"

Stepping back from the door I told him:

"I'm just fine, Captain, considering I've been in this shit box for nine days now and I didn't do a goddamn thing except protect myself!"

He motioned once again for me to come closer. Then he looked up and down the hallway to make sure that no one else was close enough to hear.

"That's what I came here to talk to you about," he said with a laugh. "I got the three little colored boys that did this shit to ya. They're locked up right now, and I'm shipping them out next week."

Pressing his face against the little window, he continued, "One is going to Sandstone, Minnesota, one is going to Marion, Illinois, and the other one is going to Hopewell, Virginia. I figure they deserve to get their asses sent to the three most redneck prisons that were available."

I felt like I had just been cheated out of my revenge. I yelled at the door, "That's all well and good, Captain. But when do I get the hell out of here?! And how did you finally figure out who it was that jumped me?!"

He told me, with his face against the little window, "Now just calm down, Timmy! Your pal George told me all about it. He came out of the chow hall just in time to see you getting jumped. George was the only son of a bitch in the yard that had what it took to come forward. I knew why the others had held back. They were going to kick someone's ass over this. I reckon he saved your ass from being shipped out of here. He also told me that he was getting bored sitting by himself until lights-out."

He paused a beat and added: "Oh yeah! I'll be letting you out today after the four o'clock count. Considering the circumstances of how things turned out, thanks to George, I was able to keep your bunk space for ya. But you'll have to be issued new clothing and new boots."

He finally shut up.

"I can live with that," I told him. "I'm just glad to be gettin' the fuck out of here. Thanks, Captain."

Later that afternoon after four o'clock count, the captain was good to his word. He released me from solitary confinement and sent me back to my unit, where I wasted no time finding my friend George. I shook his hand and thanked him at least half a dozen times.

"I couldn't leave my partner locked up," George said. "Besides that, if someone hadn't gotten this mess straightened out, there was fixing to be an ass-stompin' riot for some payback for what those little fuckers did to you. Then all of us would've been locked down for at least three days, and you and the rest of us would have gotten our butts shipped out to God knows where."

Slapping him on the shoulder, I said, "Thanks, George, you really did save my ass."

"Fuck that," George said. "I needed a gin partner."

CHAPTER SEVENTEEN

The bright lights in my unit were turned off, and the night-lights were left on. This Saturday was a special day. Rolly and I had made arrangements to play racquetball with Richie. Richie was a guy I had met years earlier while I was in the county jail in Sarasota, Florida. The US Marshals had transferred me there while the Fort Myers jail prepared an entire cell block for all of us federal inmates awaiting sentencing. By pure luck, Richie and I wound up getting assigned to the same prison. Richie had been busted while trying to smuggle eight hundred pounds of high-quality marijuana by sailboat from his home country of Belize to Port Charlotte, Florida. He was given eight years for his failed attempt. "There's no way I'm going to do eight years," Richie told me in county jail. Shaking his finger at me, he added, "If my custody level is ever reduced to one-out, the first time they put me to work outside the gate, my ass will be gone."

Three years passed and there we were, playing racquetball in prison together. Halfway through our game, the three of us took a break and Richie quietly reminded me of that very conversation.

Every six months your behavior was reviewed by your "team"—which included your counselor, your inmate case manager, and various other prison bureaucrats—and if it was deemed satisfactory, your custody level was reduced. Custody levels were originally determined at the time of your sentencing. They were based upon the severity of your crime and your culpability, and determined which level prison you would be sent to. In both of our cases, it was determined that we would be set at level three-four.

There were four levels of custody. One-out was the lowest level a con could achieve. That made you eligible to be housed at a military facility such as Eglin Air Force Base. The closest thing they had to a fence with razor wire there was a line painted in the middle of the driveway, and they told you, "Don't cross that line!"

The next level was a one-two. That put you in a minimum-security facility. They had the razor-wire-topped fences, but there were no gun towers and there was no controlled movement.

Level three-four was next, which was where we were.

Level five-six was the top. At that level you're housed in a maximum-security facility. There they didn't always use the razor-wire-topped fences. Some of those facilities had a forty-foot-high concrete wall on which guards were perched like vultures in a tree with high-powered rifles.

As you earned your way down the levels of custody, you were either transferred out or remained where you were until such time that a space became available. Prisoners are constantly being shipped around the country, as well as being released or dying. It isn't until one of those three happens that a space becomes available. This particular day, Richie had been given one-out status. While waiting to be transferred, he would start a job mowing grass and trimming bushes outside the fences. Remember earlier when I told you there were only two ways a con could get out of here—you either did the time or you died?

Well, I take that back. There was one other way, and Richie was going to take it.

Later that evening a bunch of us guys were sitting out in the yard bullshitting when Richie came up to me and handed me his Timex Ironman wristwatch.

"I figured you could use this, Tim," he said. "I don't need it anymore."

Then with a crooked smile my friend explained why.

"I'll be getting a nicer one," he said with a wink.

He walked around the yard the rest of the evening, giving away his tennis shoes, sweatshirts, racquetball racket, and a few other seemingly insignificant throwaways, which, by our meager standards, were luxury items. I interpreted his behavior to mean one thing: that night would be his last one here. It was customary for a guy to give away his stuff the day before he was legitimately released. On that day, you were given a "walk around" pass, which allowed you to move around without controls. This was the BOP's way of giving you a taste of freedom before you're thrust back into society. Richie, however, was not scheduled to be released. I knew what he was planning. I walked up behind him and put my hand on his shoulder. He turned around and gave me a bear hug and said, "Take care of yourself, brother. I love ya, man."

It wasn't until the next afternoon that any of the guards realized Richie was gone. He had shown up for his work detail that morning at seven and was counted out the back gate along with the other trustees. But it wasn't until they finished counting the inmates back inside later that day in preparation for the four o'clock count that they discovered he had escaped. By then, he had an eight-hour head start on these pricks. When central control was notified of the short count, the escape alarm was sounded and the rest of us were immediately returned to our units and locked down.

I couldn't get the smile off my face as I marched back to my house. The guards immediately began a bed book count. We were told to sit on our bunks and, when asked, state our name and ID number. The guards then matched our faces to our pictures in that book, which also corresponded to our bed assignments. That was their way of finding out which face was missing.

While the prison remained in lockdown, only one unit at a time was released to have chow and then sent right back under heavy guard. Lockdown continued this way for two more days while they searched for Richie. All work and recreation time was suspended. Richie had unintentionally given us all a vacation as a parting gift. He was never found, and after three days, prison life went back to its normal routine. George and I had our card games every night, and everyone else went about their own business.

About a month later, one of the cons from Richie's old unit received a postcard featuring gentle waves lapping up onto a white sand beach somewhere in Belize. All it said was "Wish you were here."

Some months later we learned through the prison grapevine how Richie had gotten away with it. He had arranged for his cousin to meet him on a back road that was just on the other side of a small wooded area about two hundred yards away from the prison. From there they drove all day and all night for three days until they were home. At that time the United States had no signed extradition treaty with Belize, which just years before had been known as British Honduras. Richie had made it. He had gone home like he promised me he would.

Several weeks after we heard how Richie had made his run for home, another escape was made, this time by a Colombian dude who worked for UNICOR, the prison industries. He had fashioned a pair of homemade wire cutters out of materials at his workstation. Then he somehow managed to get them past the guards and back to his unit.

The following day, which was a Saturday, his unit was the first to be released for breakfast. But instead of going to breakfast, he headed out to the lower compound of the rec yard and proceeded to cut his way through the fence. He chose a section where the old vehicle entrance to the prison used to be. Let me explain. In the early 1990s, the federal correctional institution where I was housed—FCI Tallahassee—was a very old institution and was undergoing a lot of changes, including some very badly needed modernization. One of these changes involved the building of a brand-new sally port. The sally port is the only entrance that allows vehicles to enter and leave the confines of the prison. The idea behind this type of entrance is to have two gates, with one closed at all times. The vehicle is allowed to enter through one gate, and it stops in front of the other. The open gate that it just passed through is then closed behind it. After the vehicle has been thoroughly searched, the gate in front of it is opened. The old entrance wasn't big enough to allow one gate to remain closed at all times. It was only as wide as the no-man's-land between the outer fence and the inner fence, about fifteen feet. So both gates had to remain open as a vehicle entered the prison. When those gates in that section of the fence were abandoned as the main entrance, the prison security force failed to fill in razor wire through that stretch of no-man's-land. This oversight created a perfect place for the Colombian inmate to crawl from one fence to the other without worrying about being tangled up in wire and getting his ass cut up.

Because it was so early in the morning and the sun was just coming up, no one noticed this clown cutting his way out. Being that it was Saturday and there was no controlled movement, hundreds of inmates were in every section of the rec yard by seven thirty. There simply were not enough guards in these areas before sunup to see him make his exit. It was also a stroke of pure luck that the guards in the gun towers and the roving patrols didn't see him. Later on I found out that it wasn't luck at all. At the moment he began to cut the fence, a few guys on the other side of the rec yard swatted a couple racquetballs at the fence and set off the "snitch wire" as a deliberate distraction.

The snitch wire is exactly what it sounds like. It's a small motion-sensitive wire that runs the entire length of the inner fence, and if you rattle the fence too much, it snitches on you. On windy days we were confined to the inner compound. The rec yard and upper compound were out of bounds because the windblown snitch wire would have the guards running around like Keystone Cops. But anyway, this wire is designed to send a signal to the control room, where an indicator light on a panel shows the monitors where along the fence contact has been made. Guards are then immediately dispatched to that section to investigate, and as a result they leave other areas unattended.

This gave the Colombian dude the break he needed. All he had to do at that point was try not to rattle the fence too much while he was cutting. As it happened, because there are only two counts per day, four o'clock p.m. and ten o'clock p.m., this guy had a nine-hour head start before anyone realized he was missing.

The escape alarm sounded one more time, and we were all locked down again. In this guy's case, however, he was caught the very next day three miles away from the prison. He was found freezing his ass off while hiding among a bunch of bushes in someone's backyard. What an idiot—this dude didn't speak a lick of English, and after making it beyond the fences he didn't even have a plan. He just wanted the hell out of there.

After Richie's successful escape and the short-lived excursion of that Colombian dude, the prison instituted a ten a.m. count on the weekends. They now had us locked down and standing at our bunks three times a day on Saturdays and Sundays. In the long run I figured it was a small inconvenience worth enduring for a fellow convict.

When the excitement finally died down, we all settled back into routines that revolved around a few new prison policies and tighter security. It was a pain in the ass and a change in our daily routines. In another life, changes would be welcomed and in most cases looked forward to. But in the day-to-day life of a convict, routine is the cement that holds that life and your sanity together. The bits and pieces of routine that did remain the same were welcomed like an old friend you haven't seen for years.

One particular escapee was a guy I'll never forget. His name was Wayne. Wayne was six years into a twelve-year bit for smuggling weed into the Florida Keys. His lengthy sentence was a result of some violence his partners had committed during their—and his—arrest. Wayne had been the warden's trustee for two years, even before I had arrived, and during those years he had the warden's ear every day. Wayne said that he and Jimmy Buffett were close friends who had grown up together. He told the warden that Jimmy owed him a favor and that, with the warden's permission, he would invite Buffett to play for the inmates. Eventually, the warden finally believed him, and as a result, three weeks before the holidays heralding the end of 1990, Jimmy Buffett and the Coral Reefer Band played for two and a half hours, jammed out and took requests from what was literally a captive audience in the lower rec yard compound of FCI Tallahassee. I don't know if Buffett's performance was worthy of a few lines in the local newspapers, but Wayne's performance certainly was. Three or four days after the excitement of the concert wore off, the escape alarm signaled another lockdown. Wayne had left the building. It was just a matter of time, I guess. As the warden's trustee, he had been given free range of the administration building and all of its offices each day, and he came and went through the front doors as he pleased. Often he and other trustees would take smoke breaks and even eat their sack lunches under the trees at a picnic table located outside the confines of the prison's fences, gates, and guards. His constant exposure to freedom had apparently provoked an irresistible desire to regain his own. Somebody said later that Wayne had called for a taxi from the phone on the warden's desk and simply walked out the front door. Unlike with Richie, for the remainder of the time I was there, not one of us heard any news of what had become of Wayne. He just vanished.

Ever since then, whenever I hear the jingling of sleigh bells, it doesn't take me back to my childhood night-before-Christmas visions of sugarplums and Santa making his rounds bearing gifts. No, my mental journey back through time now stops abruptly on that particular Christmas day with an image of the pissed-off warden making his way from unit to unit and inmate to inmate, rattling a half dozen or so cell door keys hanging from a large steel ring. It had always been his custom to personally hand out gifts of a chocolate bar and a handshake. It was a hollow sentiment to say the least, and not one of us gave a shit about the guy because . . . well . . . he was the fucking warden. However, this year his Merry Christmas greetings were noticeably lacking their usual seasonal enthusiasm.

CHAPTER EIGHTEEN

The previous few weeks had gone by rather quickly for me, but for George they just dragged on. The next day, he would go before the parole board one more time. He was one nervous son of a bitch. He told me that he wasn't as nervous about going in front of the board as he was about what the hell he would do if he were released. I found this a little hard to comprehend.

"What the hell do you mean?" I asked.

He couldn't answer me, so I answered for him.

"You'll say good-bye to this fuckin' place. Mary will pick you up and take you to her house. You can stay with her family for a while until you get on your feet. You'll get a job, maybe something part-time to start with, and you'll leave this nightmare behind."

He looked at me with a deer-in-the-headlights expression.

"Timmy, I don't expect you to understand this, but there'll come a day when you will. I've been locked down for half my life."

His eyes began to water.

"Everything I know right now is trapped behind these fences.

Every time I go before those guys, I find myself hoping that they'll deny my release."

His eyes dried up, his voice became angry, and a scowl formed on this gentle man's face.

"Everyone I ever knew has gone on with their lives and forgotten about me except for Mary. All the friends I have in the world are right here with me now."

I had known George for almost four years now, and I had never seen him like this. He was always the rational one. He was always so calm and collected.

"George, I'll always be your friend no matter what. When I get out of here, I'll be there no matter where you are. Maybe then I'll finally beat you at this fucked-up card game."

We both laughed halfheartedly, and his face went blank, as if someone had flipped a switch.

"Just get some rest," I said. "Don't give this shit another thought tonight if that's possible. Let's just wait and see how things turn out tomorrow."

It took me a while to get settled down that night, and I'm almost sure that George didn't get settled down at all.

The next morning he was up before the day began. He was clean-shaven, his hair was combed, and he wore his best prison khakis. When the lights came on, everyone else began moving about the unit, getting ready for his day. I strolled down to George's cubicle, shook his hand, and gave him a hug, telling him good luck, and headed off to breakfast, then on to work.

When I got to my desk, I rolled my chair back next to Dennis and began confiding in him about my concern with how strange George was acting.

"It seemed almost like he doesn't want to get outta here," I said.

Dennis turned to look over his shoulder and explained it to me.

"He's been institutionalized. Trust me on this, Timmy. When guys like George and I have been down for as long as we have, you can't help it."

His eyebrows lowered, and he looked serious as he challenged me.

"Think about it! You've spent years in here learning how to turn off your life on the outside, haven't you?"

I squinted my eyes as I figured where he was headed.

"Yep."

"And you remember how hard that was?"

"Yeah, Dennis, I do"

"Now, reverse that, Timmy, and imagine doing it all over again on the outside. It's not as easy to turn it back on as you might think."

He had turned to face me, fully engaged.

"One day, God forbid, you and I might experience the same thing."

I had never known Dennis to be particularly religious.

"Listen to me," he continued, bearing in. "This isn't something you can help him with. If, by the grace of God, he's granted his release today, this is something he'll have to do on his own."

I nodded my head with a notion of understanding and slid my chair back to my desk. This would definitely be a long day.

The hands on the clock finally aligned themselves to three thirty. I couldn't wait to get back to George's cubicle to find out about the hand that the grace of God Dennis was talking about had dealt him.

When I got there, he had already begun his afternoon ritual. The same meticulous sequence of events that he had performed every afternoon starting years before I had first set eyes on him. He had returned to his cubicle, taken out his dentures, and gently placed them on top of his locker. With the gracefulness of a safecracker he dialed the combination to his lock and opened his locker, revealing the neatly folded stacks of T-shirts, socks, and other closely guarded items. He undressed and neatly hung his clothes on a hanger. Without missing a beat he wrapped a towel around his waist, gathered up the soap and shampoo, slipped into a pair of flip-flops, and headed to the shower.

He showered, returned to his cubicle, dressed, and combed his hair. He gently picked up his teeth from atop the locker and slid them back into his mouth. The whole time, he never said a word.

I watched most of this finely choreographed ritual and smiled.

"What the fuck happened today?" I finally shouted.

With his back to me, I could barely make out the words.

"They're turnin' me loose."

My voice could be heard above all the other voices in the building.

"Ho-ly shit!"

I spun him around and screamed those words over and over and jumped up and down, grasping the front of his shirt in my two fists.

"When are you leavin'?"

In his usual calm voice, but sporting a not-so-sure-of-himself smile, he told me.

"One week from today."

I was so happy for him I couldn't hold back tears of joy. Fuck everyone else! I just let that shit go.

Before long, everybody in the unit was cramming into his cubicle to shake hands with the old-timer who was on his way out. When someone was released, especially a very well-liked and respected old-timer like George, everyone took part in the celebration. This was one of the only times in prison when all the cons shared the same feeling.

Most of the guys in prison couldn't give a shit about one another. But when a con within your own group came up for release, it was a time of joy and, in a way, a time of sadness. On one hand, you couldn't be any happier for the guy who was leaving. But on the other hand, you knew that it might be years before you saw that person again, or maybe you never would. I knew in my heart that I would one day see George again because I had promised him I would. But for the time being, I wanted to stay in a joyful place and try, over the course of the next week, to keep him in that place as well.

After dinner, George, Rolly, and I spent the evening out in the yard, talking about our lives on the outside and how quickly things can change in just a few years and, in George's case, how things had changed dramatically. As I said before, it's not easy to bring yourself to talk about these things, but under the circumstances, with George leaving and all, it seemed like the right thing to do. By doing this we thought we could help him get at least one foot outside the gate. We talked about a lot of different things, how cars had changed, how there were shopping malls with every different kind of store you can think of in them and the food courts. Oh my God, the food courts! Imagine, being able to walk up to any one of them and ask for whatever your heart desires. I had only been there three and a half years, and that sounded fantastic to me. I could only imagine what George must be thinking. It had been nearly thirty-two years since he'd walked among others as a free man.

As we talked, he seemed to loosen up a little bit. But there was still an air of sadness about him. Every now and then he would get that distant look in his eyes, and I knew he was somewhere other than here with us. Rolly and I knew it was going to be a tough week. I also knew that the prison system's bullshit reorientation program wasn't going to do him a damn bit of good. It was the Bureau of Prisons' half-assed way of preparing a guy for the streets after they have spent years breaking his spirit. Prison is supposed to be a place of rehabilitation. But that, in my opinion, is just an illusion cleverly orchestrated for the benefit of Mr. and Mrs. Joe Blow taxpayer. If there was anything I learned in my years of being locked up in there, besides how to study law, it was how to watch my back, sleep with one eye open, and fight for my life when necessary. I also learned how to rob a bank, make twenty-dollar bills, steal cars, hustle for money, and make wine. These are just a few items from a laundry list of other criminal activities available for study. I've always been a firm believer in the notion that constant exposure leads to a certain amount of contamination, which, in this case, was a fact. Prison was not a place where a guy could genuinely reflect on the behavior that had brought him there. Nor was it a place where he could truly make a conscious effort to change that behavior. Each and every day in prison demands a constant focus on your own survival. Any reasonably intelligent individual figures this shit out after being there only one day. And if not, he'll get an education all right. Rehabilitation? Fuck that shit, don't even get me started.

Sorry, enough about that.

CHAPTER NINETEEN

Life in prison can be summed up this way: the same shit, just another day. But that's exactly as it should be. Your days must be full, and you must have a routine. The trick to doing time is learning how to stay busy. You have to find something to do with every minute of your day; otherwise you'll go slap-fuckin' crazy. Routine is the key to sanity. Don't give your mind the chance to wander outside the fences.

I was reminded of a polar bear I once saw at a zoo when I was a kid. All it did was pace back and forth in the little polar bear world that its captors had created. I can see in my mind's eye where it had worn the paint from the floor, having traced its every step back and forth, back and forth. Now I understood. That was its routine. This poor creature had found a way to have a little bit of control over its life in a world where that life was totally controlled by others.

I continued with my own routine and retraced my own footsteps by being counted through the gate to get to work every evening. On one occasion as I walked toward the education building with the others, Tommy, one of the cons who ran the regular library, strolled up next to me.

"Come and see me a little bit later. I have something for you," he said.

Knowing Tommy, it could have been just about anything. Halfway through our evening shift, things started to slow down a little bit. I figured now was as good of a time as any to go and see what he had for me. When I stepped through the door of Tommy's office, he was sitting behind a desk with his feet up. In the chair next to him sat his partner in crime, Mick. He also had his feet on the desk. They looked up at me, and both of them were sporting shit-eating grins on their faces and coffee mugs in their hands.

"Care for a cup?" Mick asked.

He handed me a mug. But the beverage they were both enjoying wasn't coffee. It was "buck," a homemade wine that they had been brewing for a week in the drop ceiling above their heads.

Buck was relatively simple to make, so a lot of the cons brewed it whenever they had a chance. All you needed was a one-gallon water jug, which every con could purchase from the prison commissary. Cons used them to carry ice water to the rec yard while working out or playing racquetball. But to make buck, you filled the jug half full with water and added a little bit of yeast that you got from one of the cons working in the kitchen. If you couldn't get the yeast, a couple of pieces of bread would do. Add some pieces of fruit that you saved from dinner and a handful of Life Savers candy for flavor and sugar. Last and most important, you needed a rubber examination glove that you bought from a con who worked in the medical office. Throw all of that shit together, then snap the rubber glove over the top. Now the only thing left to do is hide it somewhere safe and let it ferment for about a week. As the week progressed, the rubber glove on top would begin to inflate from the gases produced by the fermentation process. The glove served a dual purpose. First, it trapped the smell so the guards didn't zero in on your brew and confiscate it. Second, it expanded until it popped off the top of the jug, which let you know that your batch of buck was done cooking and ready to drink.

So I took the cup, pulled up a chair, put my feet up on the desk, and had a drink with these two clowns. Tommy and Mick were a couple of Canadians, affectionately referred to as Canucks. They had gotten themselves caught stealing cars and transporting them across state lines while on vacation here in the States. That little stunt earned them each a five-year sentence.

Tommy was in his late thirties. He was about six feet tall and skinny. He wore his jet-black hair combed to one side like Hitler. His face was pockmarked, and he always had a goofy grin on it. Mick, on the other hand, was probably in his midthirties, chubby, and stood only about five feet tall. His hair was snow white, and his face was beet red. He always looked like someone had just smacked the shit out of him. But he was a happy sort of guy, and when he laughed, his eyes would get big and wide and his mouth would go to one side. The look on his face when he laughed was the one you might expect to see if the rubber-gloved Dr. Jelly Fingers was playing marbles with his prostate. These two guys were joined at the hip. They were always doing crazy shit together. Don't misunderstand me—they weren't sissies, and they weren't poking their peckers into each other's whiskers. What I meant was they just didn't seem to have a care in the world. They were always laughing and joking about something or other, and to look at them and hear them, you would think they didn't even realize where the hell they were.

The three of us sat there telling jokes and cracking one another up. Every now and then we would hide our mugs among the books when the guard walked by to check in on us. After the third mug, even I forgot where I was, and for that short time, I wasn't in prison. We could have been three good buddies sitting around the house, having a few drinks and a few laughs. The three of us got shitfaced in about an hour. Then it was time to get our act together and get ready to go back to our unit. The wine we were drinking had a very strong odor and an even bigger kick. So when we walked past the guards, it was important for us to remember to hold our breath. It was just as important to remember to put one foot in front of the other or risk falling flat on our faces and getting busted. I decided that the best thing for me to do would be to go back to my unit and enjoy the buzz in the safety of my bunk.

The ten o'clock count came and went. I woke up the next morning a little more drunk than I had been before I went to bed. I didn't remember a whole lot about what went on the night before. I didn't even remember playing cards with George—the reason being that buck has the tendency to continue fermenting as it sits in your stomach. Thank God it was Saturday morning and I could sleep in, for a little while anyway. I didn't want to miss breakfast. I had to get something in my stomach and kill this buzz before it turned into a four-alarm hangover and kicked my ass.

It's amazing the kind of things a guy can get himself into in prison. It's the last place on earth you would expect to find not only alcohol but also weed, cocaine, or even pills, but you absolutely could. Basically, if you wanted it and could afford it, you could get it.

Dennis once told me about a little racket he had going a few years back selling pot. He would have a buddy on the outside tightly wrap and tape the weed to the shaft of an arrow. Then at night, while standing in a wooded area a couple hundred yards away from the prison, the friend would shoot the arrow over the fences. If his aim was true, and it always was, the arrow would land in the soccer field that was located in the upper compound. In the morning, Dennis would have a couple of guys from whichever unit let out first go directly to the soccer field, find the arrow, and sit next to it. While sitting out in the field, appearing to be stretching and exercising, they would remove the weed from the arrow's shaft, stash it in their shoes, then bury the arrow right there. Dennis said that over the years, there were probably a hundred arrows buried in that field. The drugs of course always found their way to him because everyone in the prison knew that it was his stuff. The guys who recovered the drugs would get paid in drugs, usually a joint or two.

A code of honor of sorts was always upheld when it came to this type of thing. If you wanted it to continue coming in, and at the time Dennis was the only one who had it figured out, you made sure it found its way to him. If it didn't, the flow of weed would stop and someone would get his legs broken, so someone was always willing to retrieve his weed after it fell from the sky.

Dennis's story reminded me of my own previous experience watching weed drop from the sky. That was before prison, though.

Five years earlier, in the mid-1980s, the marijuana industry was evolving and adapting to law enforcement's pitiful attempts at interdiction. Every now and then, a throwback from the days of George Jung—the infamous cocaine smuggler from the 1970s and '80s—would literally appear above our heads in the form of an out-of-work, ex–Vietnam pilot flying an overloaded DC-3 packed with weed.

There were two separate and very distinctive categories of weed coming out of Colombia in those days, highland and lowland. These guys flew in with a load of grade-A, number-one Santa Marta Red (or Punta Roja) from the mountainous region of Santa Marta in the north. It was made up of dark-red, almost black, chunky little nuggets with the aroma of cedar and hash. This stuff had a powerful piney taste and was very expansive in your lungs. It was cultivated at higher altitudes that were cooler, less humid, and harder to get to. That's why the pilots flew it out in the smaller Cessnas and the DC-3s. The majority of what we took aboard was Colombian Red (or Red Bud), a less powerful and more commercial lowland strain. It was cultivated in the grassland or near the coast of Guajira Peninsula, which was why it arrived aboard yachts and freighters.

The Colombian locals who lived scattered throughout the mountains could only grow a relatively small amount of marijuana and typically only during the summer months. The farmers took more care growing this particular strain in order to limit the number of male plants, thus increasing the potency. The Santa Marta Red was rare, desirable, and expensive. Those smugglers bought that stuff for forty to sixty dollars a pound, compared to the ten to sixteen dollars a pound I paid for the lowland red. The more potent the smoke, the less product you need to buy. The more expensive the product is to get, the more money you can charge to sell. The more money you can charge, the more profit there is to make. The substantial profits were worth the risks. This is where the DC-3 came into the plan. It was dubbed the "workhorse of the sky," and it was the perfect size. Those guys bought up to three tons of that stuff because usually that was all the locals could pull together at any one time. Plus, small planes have cargo weight limitations.

Around the mid-1980s, the law had relaxed its grip on Miami and tightened it on southwest Florida. New air- and ground-based radar installations were used to scour the sky and the waters off our coast. With all those defenses in place, if the pilots didn't feel safe flying into Florida's air space and landing to unload, they didn't have to. They could just make a deal with me.

Four of us were aboard the F/V (fishing vessel) *Lady Miss* about seventeen nautical miles south of Marco Island. We were drifting silently two hundred yards outside of Fakahatchee Pass and just south of White Horse Key. She was a forty-foot crab boat from Marathon Key, which is part of the coral cay archipelago known as the Florida Keys. Her captain and crew were working out of Goodland, a little fishing village only six very quick nautical miles from where we were burnin' a fat one and kickin' back.

As the sun came up, its warmth lifted a light mist that hovered just above the water. The surface was so slick and calm that you couldn't make out where the ocean ended and the sky began. Around nine a.m., Steve, one of the crewmen, sat up excitedly and said, "I think I hear it!" I shushed him and closed my eyes tightly, pursed my lips and listened intently for that unmistakable sound of a plane engine. We launched ourselves from the wheelhouse out onto the deck and looked south to see her coming in low and fast. In those days, if you flew low enough, you could literally fly under the radar and, in effect, disappear. The plane had been flying at this dangerously low altitude since it entered Florida's air space, and with those two 1200-horsepower Pratt & Whitney Twin Wasps at full throttle, that bad bitch was screaming. Just then, visions of Darrel plunging from the sky in his little Cessna came flooding back as this thing suddenly dove for the deck. He leveled off at an altitude of about one hundred feet, then made his first run straight toward us. Two guys in jumpsuits wearing vintage leather flight helmets and dark-shaded goggles stood in the open cargo bay door as the plane roared past. They leaned out of the opening and hung on to a suicide strap looped around the wrist of one hand, waving to us with the other. We could see their smiling faces and hear them screaming . . . "YAHOO!" . . . as the pilot dipped each wing, bidding us hello before he slipped back up above the trees and banked to make a wide turnabout. That was just a practice run that left behind only the heavy odor of spent aviation fuel and a chill down my spine. The next time they descended and leveled off, those two clowns kicked three stacks of bales from the doorway in rapid succession. Like flat rocks being cast across a smooth pond, the bales skipped and tumbled several times across the crystal-blue water. With every impact each piece gave off brief, fireworklike explosions of brilliant white sea foam before losing momentum in a wash. Our captain, a friend of mine who really needed the work, throttled his bad boy up, and we swooped in on the first line of floating bales. Each one had a length of nylon line, the same type that we used for our traps, with a neon-yellow Styrofoam buoy attached. All we had to do was run down this string of square grouper and pull the bales aboard as if they were crab traps. The *Lady Miss* was equipped with dual pullers on the stern, which made bringing them aboard a breeze. While we pulled up the first sixty bales, those aerial bandits flashed past us once again and dropped two more bundles of twenty, which made a total of one hundred bales.

From start to finish, the entire off-load took a grand total of two minutes. Then, as quickly as they had arrived, the planes flew off into the distance. Those "Santa Marta Maniacs" had successfully dropped 6,000 pounds of weed from an aircraft designed to carry a maximum load of 6,570 pounds. That was cutting it close!

The stuff was obviously well wrapped in anticipation of the method of delivery, so there were no worries about it getting wet. At sixty pounds apiece and all the same size and shape, the bales were easy to get off the deck and stowed neatly below and out of sight. With all that excess weight in our forward and midship holds, we were now noticeably bow-heavy in the water. In anticipation of this we had brought along four dozen fish boxes, which we assembled and stacked forward on deck just behind the wheelhouse. While this preparation was under way, the captain took us to a nearby line of traps that he had set out just three hundred yards offshore a week in advance. The only thing left to do was to pull those traps, then stack them around and on top of the boxes. That bit of subterfuge made it appear that we were bringing several hundred traps home. The end of our stone crab season coincided with the fall harvest in Colombia, and everyone was bringing traps to the hilt. It also left us with some freshly caught crab claws to take to the fish house to complete the deception. Once the boxes were covered with a layering of traps, we made our run back to the dock. In broad daylight we took our load of "traps" north eight miles and right through Coon Key Pass into the sleepy fishing village of Goodland. The plan was to wait until after dinner and after dark to unload.

This crew had a rented house at the water's edge with an attached piece of land useful for storing and preparing their traps for next season. It was important for us to stay near the boat, so we hung around the house. The guys did their laundry, made lunch, and killed time and burned off some nervous energy. Mostly we took turns bullshitting with one another from across the house, pausing only to recover from the occasional outbursts of laughter.

I caught my breath after that last bout of laughter, and things quieted down a bit except for the rumbling coming from the washer and dryer. I relaxed into a smile as the noise lulled me into a daydream and to a time in the early days when I was living in my recently acquired thirty-foot-by-nine-foot Airstream estate. It took up one space in a half-moon-shaped trailer park that only had eight spaces, each one wrapped by the island's natural mangrove forest. One of those spaces belonged to Miss Jackie, the owner. She also owned the building directly across the street, which served as Chokoloskee's post office/laundromat.

Anyway, I told the story of a lazy sunny Sunday morning when Todd and Sambo dropped by for a wake 'n' bake and to hang out while they did their laundry. It was the first home I'd ever purchased, and I owned it free and clear with plenty of cash to spare. Those were the early days when I was just getting started and using a shaving kit for a wallet. The Airstream was a little cramped inside, but I was proud of it despite its size and the fact that my new Sony thirty-one-inch TV was larger than the oven in the kitchen/dining room/living room. We got toasted; then Todd and Sambo finished with the dryers so that I could dry my shit. I walked across the street and emptied my two washing machine loads into two dryers, then fed them a handful of quarters. Miss Jackie came through the door at the same time I was leaving, and we exchanged good mornings as we passed. She always cleaned up behind us and wiped things down like a mother hen. We all liked her, and she liked us. When I went back to my trailer, the three of us started laughing hysterically for about five minutes straight. Todd was recounting a time when the three of us were in a Miami strip club, trying to pelt our dancer off the stage with wadded-up ten- and twenty-dollar bills. We were there celebrating having just gotten paid, and the manager didn't have enough small bills to change our $60,000 in twenties into ones and fives. Our dancer had the face of a Shih Tzu, and we were trying to drive her ugly ass off the stage. We would then snatch up the hot little dancer on the other side of the bar and have her dance for us instead. Our strategy backfired when this dog realized what she was being pelted with and decided to stick around. That's when Todd said "Fuck it" and went around to little miss hot chick's side of the bar and handed her $500. Just a bit insulted, Miss Shih Tzu gathered up her balls of cash like so many doggy treats and scampered away. She didn't just leave the room; she left the building. The hot-ass chick was watching the whole thing, and when the pooch left, she abruptly turned, then danced and wiggled her way over to us. Now she was the only dancer in the club at one o'clock on a Sunday afternoon, and she was dancing right in front of us. This maneuver didn't go over too well with the only other five patrons in the club. They were left sitting all alone on the other side of the room with their dicks in their hands. Sambo heard it before Todd or I did: one of the assholes on the other side of the room shouted something at us. It was just barely audible over the music, but it didn't matter what the guy was saying. The fight was on.

Ah, the good old days.

The laughter was getting louder inside my little bread box, and it was getting equally as foggy, and then someone knocked on the door. When I opened it, my trailer belched a huge cloud of smoke into the front yard. When the smoke cleared, I was left standing there smile-locked and red-eyed, and it was painfully obvious that this was some great shit. Miss Jackie stepped back and waved one hand in front of her nose and clutched a fist full of cash in the other. She coughed out the words "Are these yours, Timmy? I found them sticking to the inside of one of the washing machines you were using." She grinned and handed me a little more than two grand in wet twenty-dollar bills. Still grinning, I thanked her and took a step backward into the cloud of smoke and closed the door. Since then, not a word about that day has ever been spoken between us.

The sun had gone down while I was finishing that story, and

after a bit of dinner we all strolled over to the *Lady Miss* and got busy. Each of us chewed on a toothpick as we stacked the traps on the hill and the bales into the back of a waiting freezer truck. Within an hour, we had watched it drive away and we were back in the house, showered and smoking another big fat doobie, just in time for dessert. It was eight o'clock on a Friday. *Miami Vice* was on. I loved that show! It always cracked me up.

Those days waiting for low-rent smugglers to get us the goods seemed so long ago when I was in prison. Whether you're trying to bring shit into a country or into a prison, there's never a lack of imagination.

A few guys tried introducing drugs into the prison a couple of different ways. One was to have visitors bring it in through the visitation room. But to get it into the prison meant shoving it up their ass in order to get it past the guards. This was called "keistering." Sometimes it worked, sometimes it didn't. Another way was kind of ingenious in its own right. Around the racquetball courts there was always an abundance of busted racquetballs lying along the fence. So on occasion, guys who were playing would whack a broken ball over the fences and out of the compound. So now there were broken balls outside the fences as well as inside. The guards never cleaned these up because it was always an inmate's job to pick up the trash no matter what it was. The trustees would pick up the broken balls outside the fences, and the cons working yard detail would pick up the broken balls inside the fences.

One day a con had the bright idea of having his brother come for a visit and deliver some pot. After parking his car in the visitor's parking lot, he would step out with a racquet and a couple of broken racquetballs stuffed with weed. He would then whack them toward the area of fence were the courts were located. Sometimes the balls made it over the fences, but it didn't matter either way. It would be a con picking them up and finding the shit inside the balls, then handing it over to the owner and getting paid for his effort. Everyone knew who the stuff belonged to from the method of delivery. It just goes to show you that where there is a demand, someone is always willing to supply it.

I pretty much just stuck to my one vice, drinking homemade wine. For some reason I was put on the list to be occasionally drug-tested. Since it was drugs that got me here in the first place, I didn't feel any great urge to tempt my fate twice.

The weekends in prison were always an easier time because we weren't restricted by controlled movement except for the guys going to and from the education building. That bit of control was necessary because only sixty convicts were allowed in the building at any given time. Just like most people on the outside with a nine-to-five workweek, we had the weekends off, too, or at least some of us did. The guys who worked in the kitchen and the guys who worked in the education building, like me, had to work one weekend on and one weekend off. When it was my turn to be off, I would spend my entire Saturday and Sunday playing racquetball. I took time off from lifting weights, which I had done all week for hours each day. Even though the weekends were a bit more relaxed, some things still remained the same. There was always count time at four o'clock p.m., and there was always lockdown at nine thirty p.m., then count again at ten o'clock, and of course the games with my pal George—for the last time.

CHAPTER TWENTY

The next morning, George and I shook hands and exchanged hugs. We said good-bye after more than three years locked up together, as 1990 drew to a close. Before I let go of him, I softly offered words of encouragement; then I made him a promise.

"From now on, George, you'll be traveling the road between who you think you are and who you can be," I told him. "The key is to find the courage and allow yourself to make the journey. I promise to come visit you, and next time we shake hands and embrace, we'll do it as free men."

He was still apprehensive about leaving, but I reassured him that everything was going to be just fine. I told him that he was being given a second chance to discover how wonderful life can be and to make those discoveries one day at a time. I held my true emotions in check as he walked up the stairs toward the door that led from this reality to the next. He pulled the door open, and just before he stepped through, he turned, winked at me, and waved good-bye. At that moment, I couldn't hold back what I had been suppressing since the day he had been granted his release.

Feeling as if the wind had just been knocked out of me, I sat down on the sidewalk where I had been standing. I crossed my legs and cradled my head in my hands and let go with a flood of the most awesome tears of joy I have ever known, mixed with the saddest. The father I had known in this life was gone.

A little while later, Rolly came up behind me and gently placed his hand on my shoulder. He knew it was time to turn the page and end this chapter.

"C'mon, buddy, let's go home."

That night after count, I lay in my bunk, wondering how I would fill this void in my life. Then, like a bolt of lightning, it hit me. I would finish the cases I was working on, then go to work on my own.

The next day I explained to Rolly what I had in mind.

"I'm going to retrace my steps and review everything that I said to anyone that would be in a position to help me."

I was determined not to be here another seven years. I also explained to Rolly how almost everyone involved in my case had cooperated with the government and had been given immunity in exchange for a lesser sentence. And for their cooperation and name-dropping, they had gotten their sentences reduced below the mandatory minimum of ten years. Many names had been given more than once, but it didn't matter. What mattered was that simply by giving these names, you confirmed to the Feds that they were getting all the right people.

"'Cooperate,' that's the key word!" Rolly said. Looking at me with one eyebrow raised, he added, "If this is ever going to work, that's the word that is going to make it happen."

I had taken the initiative to learn about our laws early during my sentence because nobody else in here would go out of his way to teach me how to navigate my way through the American legal system. I told myself that it was essential to have a comprehensive understanding of law if anything significant was going to come out of being down here. It also became painfully obvious that if you don't have that understanding, like most inmates here, you just find yourself banging your head against another of our prison system's brick walls. On one side of the wall were all the legal answers I sought. On the convicts' side, however, we had no idea how to break through and get those answers. Everything I had ever gotten myself into goaded me into a thirst for more. Integrating that form of posturing into my life is ultimately how I wound up here. So it seemed only natural that I pursue this course of action and quench this latest intolerable thirst. But beyond all of that, at this stage of the game, everyone could kiss my ass. I could afford to be self-important. Law had become an obsession. They say that constant exposure leads to a certain amount of contamination. In this case I was saturated from head to toe. Rolly and I both had earned associate's degrees in paralegal studies through a correspondence course from the University of Honolulu. We didn't do all that work just to sit there and take it in the ass.

Week after week, I pored over case law, and week after week, Rolly was right there with me. He was now as determined as I was to beat this sentence. When we weren't working out or playing racquetball, we were side by side researching and discussing numerous relevant points of law. We looked for cases of precedents that were on point to mine and based on cooperation with authorities. Rolly lived in a different unit, so it wasn't possible for him to help me fill the void I now felt between ten o'clock count and lights-out. So I decided to use that time to read books and escape that fucking hole, if only for a little while.

Our time spent together over the next several months wasn't all about me. It was also about Rolly and how counterfeiting twenty-dollar bills had made him rich and ultimately made him the property of the US government.

"Using the counterfeit bills isn't what ultimately got me caught," he told me. "It was the amount of cash I was spending. They didn't know for the longest time that the bills were homemade. When you're making money—I mean literally making money—you really have only one goal in mind and that is to spend it."

He told me he was traveling all over the Northeast, buying all sorts of things. A lot of things that he bought he kept. But the majority of the stuff, like appliances and other household goods, he would turn around and sell at a super discount in order to have clean money. I told him that I had experienced the same problem.

For me, trying to come up with new ways of spending or even getting rid of the money was always a challenge. But in a lot of ways it was kind of fun. There are only so many houses you can buy and so many cars you can buy. That's when your money starts to become obvious and people raise an eyebrow. When it gets to that point, you begin to piss it away on things that don't accumulate. For instance, you go to a bar and buy drinks and champagne for all your friends and everyone else who happens to be there at the time.

This sort of behavior was not out of the ordinary for guys like us. The owners of the nightclubs we would frequent were friends of ours. They certainly weren't going to turn our business away, even if we did get a little bit rowdy at times. After all, we were each spending thousands of dollars a night. Once the word got out that we were there, people would just start showing up to party. I rambled on about my glory days outrunning the law and making more money than I could spend until my brain turned to mush. I told Rolly I had had enough for one day and that I was going back to my unit to take a nap.

A couple of hours later, I was awakened from my nap to participate in the ritual of four o'clock count. After the count I got back on my bunk and waited to be released for dinner. During that time every day, the guard came back into the unit to announce mail call. It was another one of those times that every inmate looked forward to, except me. One time when I was talking to my brother during a jailhouse phone call, he told me, "If Mom ever asks if I've written to you, tell her that I have."

Hearing him say those words disillusioned me. The unlikely prospect of receiving mail made me feel more isolated. Comments like that helped transform my heart into a rock that much quicker. However, my grandmother Ruth had written to me once, and I must have read her letter over and over at least a hundred times. She wrote very specifically about our family's history, not only on her side, which was my father's, but on my mother's side, too. In retrospect, I think she was subtly telling me how a family tree will grow a few branches that the older generations would prefer to see trimmed. It looked as though every hundred years or so, someone in my family grew a pair of balls and stepped up to do what at the time seemed simply the right thing to do. My great-grandpa Albert Danals, father of Grandpa Leslie Everett Danals, on my mother's side, was a man very much involved in coordinating and operating the Underground Railroad in Ontario, Ohio, where he successfully smuggled thousands of blacks out of slavery in the South to freedom in the North. My mother would tell me she could remember hearing the stories of a railroad that was running through her grandpa's barn, but for all of her exploring she could never find the tracks for the trains.

One branch of my family tree could have used a bit of trimming. This branch also sprouted from my great-great-grandfather, who happened to fall in love with and marry Martha Viola Harding, a first cousin to a brilliant up-and-coming newspaper publisher, Warren G. Harding. History records my great-great-granduncle as having been the twenty-ninth president of the United States, and it also records him as having been responsible for running one of the most corrupt presidencies in US history. He died suspiciously of a cause undetermined. Upon hearing word of her husband's sudden demise, First Lady Florence (my great-great-grandaunt Flo Harding) is noted for having been Johnny-on-the-spot in that she immediately began burning all the now late president's personal files.

I think that Grandma Ruth was trying to tell me that only time and history could judge whether a person had made the proper choices in life. Sometimes a person's behavior at the time seems just and right to him. So he puts his head down and lives that life, only to look up one day to find out that history has made its own judgment and society has pinned a label on him. I never told Grandma how much that letter meant to me and how many times the unconditional love that I sensed in her written voice brought me back from the brink of insanity. And if she ever reads this, a very personal page in my life story will have come full circle. I always knew that I had disappointed her. But regardless of what I've done to my life, she never stopped communicating with me. Nevertheless, the false excitement and the remote possibilities of my ever receiving another letter always haunted me.

Ten or so names were called; then the guard yelled, "McBride!"

I jumped from my bunk, ran to collect my mail, and wondered with each step who had written to me. With letter in hand I quickly read the name and return address: "Mary Burke, Talladega, Alabama." Right away I figured it must be a letter from George. Being that ex-cons were not allowed to communicate with cons still in prison or on parole, he must have disguised it as a letter from Mary. But when I opened it and began to read, I realized that it was, in fact, from Mary. She wrote that she was sorry to have to tell me this, but George had been arrested once again.

My heart jumped up into my throat, and it was hard to catch my breath as I read on. She tried in her own words to describe to me what had taken place, but stopped and wrote instead, "I've enclosed an article from the local newspaper that will tell you everything you need to know."

My hands shook as I removed a newspaper clipping from the envelope. The headline read, "Recently Paroled Bank Robber Picks Up Where He Left Off."

Tears obscured the words that I could barely read. The clipping went on to say:

> *George ——— had been recently released from federal prison on parole. After serving thirty-one years of a thirty-eight year sentence, he decided to give up his new job as an antique furniture refinisher to, once again, pursue a life of crime. He had acted alone in perpetrating one of the most daring bank robberies in recent times.*

The more I read, the more this story began to sound all too familiar.

> *The robbery had taken place over the Fourth of July weekend. His obvious knowledge of this type of crime allowed him to disable the alarm system including security cameras and motion*

sensors. Gaining access through the roof he removed the contents of every safety-deposit box in the vault room then quietly slipped away undetected.

This next part shocked me and I will never understand it as long as I live.

As the FBI agents conducted their investigation of the crime scene, they came across a set of dentures that had been carefully laid on top of a row of safety-deposit boxes. A simple visual inspection of the teeth revealed a number stamped on the underside of the upper plate. That number was then traced back to the Bureau of Prisons. A printout of the records indicated that the dentures were in fact prison issue. Next to the same number that was stamped on that set of teeth was my old friend's name, in bold ink. His long-standing routine of taking them out (and setting them on top of his locker) before opening a little metal door had betrayed him. Or had it? Did he leave them there on purpose? Did he want to get sent back to prison? These are the questions that will haunt me until the day I die.

I spent the next few days going in and out of the throes of grief and disbelief. I read the article over and over again, hoping that by some miracle the storyline would change. I now knew more than ever that I had to get the hell out of prison. There are ways to beat the system, but that's not what usually ends up happening. The system always beats you back.

Dennis was one of these continuous pains in the Bureau of Prisons' ass. He was notorious for carpet bombing them with dozens upon dozens of frivolous written complaints, and he knew the staff had to answer each one individually. This was his way of rebelling against a system he despised. I have to credit Dennis with having inspired a lot of us to tell our own stories. He was a one-of-a-kind man who gave out hope like it was candy from his pocket. From behind prison fences and walls, he wrote a novel called *The Getbacks of Mother Superior*, which was published by Arbor House in 1987. The story's protagonist robs banks while well armed and dressed like a nun, hence the name. The book is an awesome tale of revenge. After getting caught, "Mother Superior" devises a most ingenious escape plan using new computers that empty out half the prison's population. In retrospect, Dennis had come up with his own "get-back" against the system. His frivolous written complaints wound up becoming a meticulously stacked pyramid of building blocks that the BOP simply knocked over. So just like that bastard redheaded, freckled-faced bully who occupies childhood nightmares, the Bureau of Prisons showed him how much they gave a shit. One chilly morning just before the holidays, Rolly and I reported to our work assignments, and as usual we were counted into the building first. This always gave us time to set up, but in this case we were told to pack up. Caught completely by surprise, which was the prison's way of doing things, we were told by the guards to box up everything belonging to Dennis Lehman. Damn! After thirty-two years he was being shipped out and relocated to a new tighter-security prison that had just opened about sixty miles west of us in Marianna. When those hacks carried those boxes down the hall and around the corner, that was the last of Dennis I ever saw.

Back at my desk and with a renewed sense of urgency, I channeled all my effort and all that I had taught myself and that Dennis had taught me over the past three and a half years toward one goal: getting a reduction in sentence based on cooperation.

I leaned over my desk with my head in my hands. I looked to the left and saw a copy of *Black's Law Dictionary*. That is the dictionary that lawyers depend on to define the wording used in the writing of any legal document. I casually flipped through the pages until I found the legal definition for the term "cooperation." That was the key. Everybody who had gotten his sentence reduced had cooperated with the government in some way. I had not cooperated—or had I? Simply put, from a legal standpoint, if someone asks you for something and you give it to them, you have, by all accounts, cooperated. That's all it took. I sat straight up in my chair.

"Holy shit, this is it!"

I handed the dictionary to my wide-eyed legal partner Rolly, who read it for himself and asked me a few questions.

"Did the investigators ask you for something?"

"Oh yes, they did!" I answered.

"And did you give it to them?"

"Hell yeah, I did!"

"OK, Tim, what exactly did you give them?"

Before I could answer that question, though, I had to tell Rolly how the Saltwater Cowboys were finally brought down. That would explain my "cooperation"—which wasn't really cooperation at all. But it might be a legal loophole big enough to drive a damn oil tanker through and leave that fucking hellhole.

CHAPTER TWENTY-ONE

In 1987 and 1988, the US government came after us hard. The Feds stepped up their so-called War on Drugs. It became increasingly difficult to smuggle our loads past them. By that time, they had stopped the flow of cocaine into Miami or at least reduced it to almost nothing in comparison to what it had been. The Cubans and the Colombians involved in the drug trade had been killing one another for years, not to mention anyone who just happened to be standing around them. *Time* magazine published an issue with the title "Paradise Lost" on the cover, naming Miami "the murder capital of the world." Other than places that were embroiled in true warfare, Miami was the most dangerous place to be at the time. That article, along with pleas from the city's officials and the citizens of South Florida, prompted our federal government to step in and help local authorities rescue the city.

Like a tsunami, a special task force, along with local law enforcement, flooded the Miami area and successfully achieved their objective. They then trained their sights on southwest Florida. They had been trying for years to catch us, and for years they had failed.

Local authorities came close numerous times, but we always managed, one way or another, to elude their grasp. They captured the odd load here and there, but the load was all they got. They never caught the men. Each night, the evening news would report on the government's success in terms of percentages. The report would go something like this:

"Drug trafficking in southwest Florida is down by twenty-five percent."

I watched that crap and always wondered how in the hell the government came up with those numbers.

They seemed to be throwing out numbers to justify the billions of dollars they were spending each year to try to stop guys like us. Without a doubt, these percentages were horseshit! For every one load that they seized, fifty or more would get past them. The people running this war knew we were still getting away with it but had no clue how much was really coming in. I was sure that fact really pissed them off. We weren't just a bunch of backwater inbred rednecks! Our crews had this operation down to a science. In order to counter their efforts, we were spending a lot of money on the latest technology available at the time. These items became the tools of our trade: color radar, starlight scopes, infrared scopes, parabolic dishes, VHF radio frequency scanners, two-meter multiple-channel radios, Polaris scanners, and other high-tech tools.

Hell, when the Polaris scanner was on, the law didn't even have to talk on the radio. When a lawman pressed the key on his radio mic, a little LED light on our scanner would strobe around the degrees on a compass. When it picked up the law's signal, the light would stop and reveal the direction of the transmission. We knew where the law was every step of the way.

Paying off an officer of the law now and then was also a useful tool. Payoffs weren't really that difficult. Think about this: If you offer a guy ten times his annual salary in cash to look the other way, what the hell do you think he's going to do? He's going to take it and look the other fucking way! I even wore a personal radio-frequency detector under my clothing. If I got within ten feet of someone with a transmitter, the device would begin to vibrate.

All of that technology at our disposal coupled with the most powerful boats money could buy gave us a huge advantage, and that pissed the law off even more.

In early September of 1987, a job to bring twenty-eight tons of Colombian Red ashore was painstakingly planned out and ready to be executed. The sequence of events had been choreographed and was now set to be put into motion. The plan had a wrinkle, however. We were going to split the load and bring it ashore at two separate locations. Half of the fifty-seven thousand pounds would go to Everglades City, and the other half to Pine Island through Boca Grande Pass just north of Fort Myers.

I let Johnny handle our crew in Everglades City while I went north with Clark and his brother-in-law to meet up with the crew on Pine Island. I knew these guys on Pine Island but had never worked with them before. I sent my own chase boat and its crew alongside their load boat to make sure things went as planned. Their off-loading crew and I met at a hotel on Pine Island to wait for a radio call that would signal us to head out and begin the night's work. Our half of the load would be packed into a large truck that would then be driven to Miami in the morning. We received the call and went down to the parking lot of the hotel, where two vehicles were waiting to take us to the off-load site. As we were leaving the parking lot, I noticed that a tan Bronco appeared to be circling the hotel. I passed it off as some Yankee who had gotten himself lost in the Florida backwaters. I didn't give it another thought. We had about a fifteen-minute drive down a backcountry road to get to our spot out in the sticks.

Turning off of the main road into an overgrown gravel driveway, our driver stopped and let us off; then he backed out and drove away. Walking farther down the gravel road through a tall pine forest, we came to a dock that stuck out into one of the back bays of Boca Grande Pass. This rickety dock peeked out just about three feet beyond the mangrove branches. The balance of its fifteen-or-so-foot length reached back to the bank where we stood. The tops of its once hearty posts were weathered and worn down like ancient cypress stumps. Rusted nails protruding from the spars and slippery moss-covered planks were the only things holding it together. But it had enough life left in it to service us one last time. This is where the mullet skiffs and the T-Crafts would come to unload their bales. Each boat crew would arrive and toss their bales onto the dock, then go back for more. The shore crew would then carry the bales to a box truck that had been skillfully backed into position through the pine trees.

The first of more than a dozen boats showed up with its bundles and tossed them off. We began to fill the truck as the second set of boats came in, and those pieces were tossed and loaded. The boats all took off across the bay and out the pass to reload. This was perfect; everything was going smoothly. Typically they would make three or four trips back and forth to the load boat until all the bales were safely onshore. The boats never showed for their third arrival, however, and they didn't respond to my repeated radio call signals. Something was not right.

Thirty minutes passed before I got a call on the radio, but it wasn't from the boats; it was from our watchman out on the main road.

"A car just pulled in here, then backed out and took off down the road again," he said.

That sounded unusual, considering we were out in the middle of nowhere. I decided at that time to walk out to the main road and check it out for myself. There was still no word from my missing boats. When I reached the road, my watchman repeated what he had said to me over the radio. Looking around, I noticed that Clark and some of the guys who were supposed to be back at the dock were standing right behind me. Seemed that they, too, were suspicious and a bit apprehensive over what was happening.

We heard what sounded like waves breaking steadily on the shore, but the sound transformed into the rumble of cars and trucks roaring down the road to our right. My cry to withdraw trumped the noise of squealing rubber as their tires gripped the pavement.

"Hit the woods, boys! We're fucked!"

When the vehicles got close enough for their headlights to illuminate the road in front of us, everybody scattered like roaches in the kitchen and took off running in different directions. Those who fled to the left had a thick pine tree forest to aid in their escape. Those who ran to the right had a thick field of three-foot-tall palmetto bushes that provided no cover at all. Unfortunately, I hightailed it for the palmetto bushes, as did a Colombian asshole who had come here illegally on one of the boats. With no time to rethink my choice of direction, I kept running. When the first vehicle came into sight, I had made it only about thirty feet into the palmettos; then I squatted down among the branches. The first vehicle to pull in was that damn tan Bronco that had been circling the hotel. That's the only one I saw before I ducked down out of sight. These guys were on us like flies on a turd. I could only assume that these pricks had been watching us from the beginning.

Even though it was dark, I could see their feet through the branches by the light coming from the other cars. All the while that damn Colombian was crunching his way through the palmettos. I winced with every crunch and crack. All I could think was, *Stop and get down, you fuckin' moron. If these guys hear you or see you, they'll trip right over me to get to you!*

Finally he stopped moving. I didn't hear anything now except the cops, or whoever they were, shouting:

"There's a few of them over there, running through the trees!"

"Get in there, boys . . . Go! Go! Go!"

Several of them took off running after my crew while others got in their cars, backed out, and took off down the road. Squealing its tires, the Bronco took off, too.

As I sat there, listening silently, I could still hear the sound of a car motor running. It was coming from out on the main road, but I couldn't tell if there was anyone in the vehicle. My legs were getting numb because I was still squatting. Somehow I had to get the feeling back in my legs. The palmetto branches were dry and—just as they did for that Colombian dickhead—they made a crunching sound every time I tried to move. So whenever one of those guys talked, closed a door, or made any kind of sound at all, I would move my legs little by little out from under me. Eventually, I managed to sit down on my ass and get the feeling back into my legs. I stayed right there for hours, all night until daybreak. I knew that if those bastards came back after sunrise, they would sure as hell see me sitting there. I was right there next to them. They could have spit on me, I was so close.

All of a sudden the Bronco came back, pulled in, and stopped right next to me again. I stayed down, as low as I could, not making a sound. The driver got out and started to walk into the woods when a voice called to him.

"Where are you goin'?"

"I'm gonna walk back in there and see what we've got," the Bronco guy answered.

"Hold on, man," the other guy said. "I'll go with you!"

Off they went into the trees toward the box truck. I couldn't see them, but I pictured them vanishing into the woods. Maybe I could make a run for it. But there remained one problem. A car was in the road, and it was still running.

I debated with myself what to do. It was getting bright enough to see in the dawn light. I had to get the fuck out of there. But if I lifted my head to look above the bushes and a cop was in the idling car, I had three options. I was either going to run him over, get busted, or get shot.

I also knew that those guys who walked into the woods wouldn't stay back there long, and I was afraid more vehicles would show up. I raised my head and peeked over the palmettos. I saw a police car—with nobody in it! I got up and ran like hell past the idling cop car, then across the road. I ran through a ditch on the other side, then ripped into a patch of thick brush and kept on going. Not once did I look back. My tunnel vision wouldn't allow it. I don't know how far I ran. I just ran like my ass was on fire and picked up my pace each time one of my feet hit the ground. Swatting at branches to keep them from hitting me in the face, I pushed myself harder and harder until my lungs were about to explode. After what seemed like miles, I stopped and dove under a patch of thick bushes, then covered myself with leaves, dirt, and anything else I could scrape up. I lay there beneath the dense jungle vegetation, trying to catch my breath and not believing I had just gotten away. My breathing and heart rate slowed as I remained there, as quiet as possible, listening for the sound of my pursuers. I didn't hear a thing. That was the most beautiful sound I never heard. I was burned out, stressed out, and freaked out. Then I passed out.

I was awakened by the sound of a helicopter flying over my head. As it flew by, the beating blades gave way to the sound of branches breaking in the distance along with a hollow banging. They were towing my box truck with about one hundred bales in it out of the trees. I dozed off again, only to wake up later on in the afternoon to a different sound that crept much closer. Slowly opening one eye, I found myself face-to-face with a full-grown panther. A living, breathing, meat-eating Florida panther. That big bastard was crouched down and sneaking up on me like I was its next meal. After running and hiding out from the law for nearly a full day, I wasn't about to let it all end in the jaws of some big pussycat. Of course, I wasn't exactly sure how I was going to get out of this precarious situation, but one thing I knew for certain was that I was tired and I was pissed off. I jumped up with my arms raised and roared like a lion. That damn cat leaped about six feet into the air and did a back flip. It landed on its feet, then shot off through the bushes like it had been fired from a cannon.

After that, there was no way I could go back to sleep because I really didn't trust that cat to stay away. It was late afternoon now, and the activity I'd heard throughout most of the day had stopped. I needed to wait until dark before making my way out of the bush.

Now that all the events of the past night and day were behind me, I breathed a small sigh of relief and began to feel a little more relaxed. I could now think clearly enough to formulate my next escape. After dark I would walk along the side of the road behind the trees in case the law was still out searching for runaway smugglers. I knew of a fish house about five miles down the road, where I would find a phone and call someone to get me the hell out of there.

But first things first. I had to take a serious dump. I hadn't relieved myself since the day before, and now there was an angry brown bear clawing at my back door. I did my business and realized that the only paper I had to wipe my ass with was the $4,000 in hundred-dollar bills I had in my front pocket. Damn, it cost me $500 to wipe my ass. That was one for the Guinness book, the most expensive shit ever taken. Of course, there was no way those bills were going back into my pocket, so I buried them right there and began to make my way back to the road.

I walked for miles, stumbling through the darkness. Just two cars passed by during my three-hour trek. One was a sheriff's car, and the other was a piece-of-shit pickup truck. I was glad I had decided to keep off the road and walk among the trees. I emerged from the woods behind the Pine Island fish house and was a bit unnerved to see that there were still lights on inside and out. I could see a phone booth in the parking lot but no people. Everybody must have been inside the fish house. I didn't want to just come out of nowhere and walk up to the phone. After all, it was two o'clock in the morning.

I stood back in the cover of the trees, plucking from my clothes the leaves, sticks, and burrs that I had acquired during my little romp through the bush. At that moment two shrimp boats pulled in and tied up to the dock. They were the reason the fish house was open at this hour. The employees had been waiting for these guys to show up so they could unload their catch.

The crews came off their boats and for a while milled around outside, taking turns using that pay phone. Presumably they were calling for a ride home. This was the opportunity I'd been waiting for. I would call for a ride as well. Stepping from the shadows, I casually strolled over and mingled with them. When my turn on the phone came, I stepped in, grabbed the phone book, and quickly looked up the number to a taxi service and dialed the first one I came to. The phone rang about a half a dozen times before my desperate call for help was answered. The guy on the other end sounded like he had just gotten out of bed. When I told him where to pick me up, the tone of his voice abruptly changed and he sounded wide-awake.

"You're where?"

Knowing full well that he had heard me the first time, I played along.

"I'm at the Pine Island fish house!"

"Man, you're hell and gone from where I am!"

That's when I told him something he never had expected to hear.

"I've been offshore shrimp fishing for the last three weeks. Start your meter running when you leave the house, and I'll give you five hundred dollars plus your fare here and the fare to my destination."

"You're not shittin' me, are ya, fella?"

"No, I'm definitely not shittin' ya!" I told him. "All you have to do is come and get my ass right now!"

No sooner had I gotten that out of my mouth than a sheriff's car showed up. Was my lucky streak about to finally run out? To my surprise he slowly cruised around the parking lot, then back out onto the street, and drove away into the night. Relaxing my grip on the phone, I let out a sigh of relief.

"What's your name, man?" I asked the taxi driver.

"Jack."

"Well, Jack, there are other guys here waiting for the phone. What's it going to be? Are you comin' or not?"

"Yeah, I'm getting dressed right now. I'll be there in a little while."

"Hustle makes things happen, Jack. So hurry every chance you get."

As I passed the phone to the next guy in line, there was nothing more I could do now except hang out with these fishermen and bullshit until my ride came.

Forty-five minutes later Jack showed up to take me to a hotel in North Fort Myers. The first thing I did when I opened the cab door was toss $500 into his lap and tell him, "You're a sight for sore eyes, Jack. Keep that meter running." I slumped into the seat. "Let's get outta here."

On the way to the hotel there wasn't much conversation between us. I was too tired. Feeling that my ordeal had finally come to an end, I began drifting in and out of sleep. The only conversation I remembered having with Jack was when he said to me, "I guess there was a little trouble out here the night before last. A few good ol' boys got their weed took from 'em."

"No shit?"

"Yep, it's been on the TV all day," he said. "They're still lookin' for 'em, though. I guess they all got the hell out of there OK."

When I got into my room at the hotel, my first order of business was to take a long hot shower. The second order of business was to climb into that big soft bed and fall right into a deep coma-like sleep. Early afternoon the next day when I finally woke up, I ordered a late lunch from room service and called a friend. That friend wasn't involved with my activities at all, which is why I chose him to come and get me.

Two days passed before any of us from the job tried to connect with one another. As far as I could tell from keeping a close eye on the news those two days, not one of my crew had been arrested. As it turned out, none were. I finally made contact with several of my main guys, and the news from them was disturbing to say the least.

Clark, his brother-in-law, and a few others who had taken the pine forest route out of there had somehow managed to make their way back to the hotel parking lot and Clark's van. Unfortunately, they wound up being detained by agents from the Drug Enforcement Administration and US Customs. After they were questioned for an hour and their vehicles were thoroughly searched, they were released. None of them could be placed at the scene of the crime, so the law had nothing to hold them on. We were in the clear, for the time being, anyway.

CHAPTER TWENTY-TWO

Several weeks later, two investigators with the Florida Department of Law Enforcement showed up at my home. They started firing a barrage of questions at me.

"Where were you on the evening of September ninth?"

They held up photographs of guys' faces. "Do you know him . . . or him?"

These guys were pissing me off, so I just stayed cool and let them play.

It was none of their goddamn business where I was that night, and unless they had a warrant for my arrest, they could kiss my ass. And if they did have a warrant, they could still kiss my ass!

I have to say, though, one of the pictures did get my attention. It was the picture of my old pal Clark, and he was standing next to his bro-in-law. Damn!

I gave my internal monologue a break and calmly told the guy holding the pictures, "Yeah, I know this guy. We went fishing together a while back. Why?"

That was when the other prick proceeded to tell me that my

wallet and checkbook were found in that guy's van, and that the van's occupants were persons of interest in an investigation into marijuana smuggling.

"What the hell has any of this got to do with me?" I was beginning to lose my cool. "So I left my things in his van, what of it? I've got them back now, thanks!"

Clearly not impressed with the brass balls I was hanging in front of their faces, one of the smart-ass detectives lashed back at me.

"Are you sure you want to stick with that story?"

"Yep! That's the only story I have!"

They walked from my doorway back to their car, and that smart-ass turned to me one last time and said, "OK then, we'll see you later. Oh, by the way, I hope you sleep well tonight."

That smart-ass that turned to speak up to me was Florida Department of Law Enforcement Special Agent David R. Waller, who just happened to be the guy in charge of this case and the mystery man driving the tan Bronco that fateful night.

During the months that followed my run through the jungle, I lost track of everyone. I never saw Clark or his brother-in-law again after that day when the law came knocking on my door. Each of us was involved to his own degree in this mess, and each of us faced individual consequences based on his culpability. These were trying times. We all knew the law was on to us now, which prompted the question: How did they finally get to us after all these years of smuggling millions of pounds right under their noses?

One afternoon I answered another knock at my door and was greeted by a chubby smiley-faced bald dude with black-rimmed glasses. This asshole wore black pants and a black tie, and he was sweating through his plain white shirt. He asked me if my name was Timothy McBride. I told him yes, but I wasn't interested in what he was selling. Giving a yellow-toothed smile and a laugh, Mr. Chuckles handed me a subpoena to appear before a US grand jury. I almost shit myself. I didn't say a word as I slammed the door in his face and beat a hasty retreat into my house. I snatched up the phone and dialed my attorney.

He and I met the next day in his office, and he told me that the only thing I could do at this point was to appear before the grand jury. My appearance was the only way we could find out what was happening. Well, I knew what was happening. I was about to get corn-holed by the US government.

My attorney and I agreed that, upon appearing before the grand jury, I should invoke my Fifth Amendment right to not answer any of the questions asked of me. When the US Attorney's Office learned of our strategy, it waived the hearing and dismissed me just as I was ready to walk into their chambers. Over the next few months my attorney collected discovery, the evidence that the US prosecutor had gathered against me. When I read through those pages, I discovered the simple reason for my dismissal from the grand jury: the US Attorney's Office already had enough evidence to indict me, and they did just that.

The government's undercover effort was known as Operation Peacemaker. It was a long and difficult investigation into marijuana and cocaine smuggling perpetrated by residents of Everglades City and the surrounding area.

Nearly a year passed after that hellish night on Pine Island. We continued to work for a few months afterward but at a much slower and more guarded pace. We were still working right up until the night I was awakened by another knock on my front door at approximately two thirty a.m. I wondered who the hell was knocking on my door at that hour. I peeked through the blinds and saw a cop standing on my front porch. Don, a friend who had been staying in one of my guest rooms, was rattled awake, too, and I turned away from the window and told him to go tell that cop I wasn't home.

My dogs had been barking, so I figured a neighbor had called the police to complain. I went back to bed, thinking that would be the end of it. Don opened the door, and as soon as it was open far enough, the cop grabbed him, pulled him from the doorway, and threw him out into the front yard. When he rolled over onto his back, he opened his eyes to the barrel of a 9-millimeter pistol resting gently against his forehead. The man holding the gun wore a mask and was clad in all black, and he was hollering in my friend's face.

"Is Tim McBride in there?"

Out of the corner of his eye, Don saw a group that looked like ninjas gathering by the garage, then slammed his eyes closed. With his eyes tightly shut, he pleaded for this black-clad ninja not to shoot him in the face.

"Oh yes, sir, he's in there all right!"

I'm pretty sure at that moment the poor son of a bitch was shitting in his boxers. From my bed I saw beams of light swirling around on the walls, floor, and ceiling in the hallway. I got up and walked to my bedroom door and poked my head around the corner. The beams of light were now aimed at my face. I stepped out into the hallway with my hands shading my eyes. A voice boomed from behind the glare.

"Are you Tim McBride?"

"Yeah, I'm Tim," I hollered back. "What the hell's going on here?"

The lights blinded me so I couldn't see who was yelling at me.

"Get those fuckin' lights outta my face!"

The next thing I heard was this command:

"Get on your knees, and put your fuckin' hands behind your head!"

Five guys blitzed me like I was an NFL quarterback, and down I went. I felt the cold steel of gun barrels against my back, neck, and head. A pile of men was on top of me. One of them pulled my arms behind my back, handcuffed me, then picked me up. Two of them led me to the living room couch, where I sat in my underwear, watching the show. My house was full of agents from the US Customs Service, Drug Enforcement Agency, Florida Department of Law Enforcement, and practically every agency from the Gulf of Mexico to Washington, DC. There were investigators from the US Attorney's Office and US Marshals Service, not to mention the Naples Trident drug enforcement task force from the Collier County Sheriff's Office and, last but not least, the Naples Police Department. They had all come for a big prize—me!

All of them spent the rest of that morning dragging me around to each of their various agency headquarters to be fingerprinted and photographed. At one point, I was placed into a holding cell the size of a closet and chained to a steel bench alongside Carlos, one of my Cuban buddies from Naples. I guess this was done because they expected Carlos and me to talk to each other. But that didn't happen. He and I weren't naive enough to think that they weren't voice- and video-recording everything we might say. After a half hour of silence we were separated. I was shackled from head to toe, then transported to the federal building in downtown Fort Myers. That's the last time Carlos's and my paths crossed for some time. Upon arriving, I was taken inside and thrown into another holding cell not much bigger than the one I had just left except I shared this one with about twenty of my coconspirators. It seemed that the law was having a busy morning. More and more guys began to arrive, and after a few hours we all stood shoulder to shoulder. A bunch of outlaws drunk on adrenaline and crowded into a tiny cell could have exploded into a brawl had we all not known one another. All that afternoon each of us was taken before a federal judge and given a personal surety bond and released on his own recognizance. There were just too many of us to hold in custody. We all went home that night and watched a replay of the day's events on national news.

At my arraignment I stood before the bench alongside five of my confederates and listened to the tyrannical ravings of US District Judge Elizabeth Kovachevich, who ruled the court. She made it clear from the start of the proceedings that she had a mission beyond her job. She didn't just want to levy justice. She wanted to punish us.

Kovachevich opened by saying, "In all of the indictments handed out, there are four counts on this one alone that carry a mandatory minimum sentence of forty years to life."

When she informed us that $4 million in fines would also be imposed, I spoke up under my breath a little too loudly.

"Jesus, why don't you go for thirty million while you're at it?"

She looked down at me from her bench and glared over her reading glasses.

"Mr. McBride, this is not funny. You young men are in serious trouble."

My attorney motioned his fingers across his throat. This was his way of telling me to shut the fuck up.

"*You* shut the fuck up!" I said to him in a harsh whisper. "If this old bag is going to give me life for this shit, she's gonna hear me out! There's more to us than this!"

I felt as if I had been pronounced guilty before proved innocent. I prepared to sacrifice myself on her altar of justice by opening my big fucking mouth when the third guy in our row chimed in. It was Teddy, an upper-level member of the crew and one of our go-to guys. Let's just say he was very much involved in everything we did and ranked right up there among the top ten craziest sons of bitches I've ever known.

"Excuse me, Your Honor," he began. "You're telling us that we're in serious trouble and that you want to give us life in prison and all these fines? We weren't shooting the place up! We couldn't get that shit in here fast enough. It wasn't like we were shoving it down anyone's throat. The minute it hit the streets, it was gone."

The other guys were bowing their heads, staring at their toes with their hands behind their backs. I had my chin up and stared into the judge's flaming eyes as Teddy continued his statement.

"There's guys in prison charged with rape or molesting children, and drunk drivers who have killed innocent families that are doing less time!"

The judge scooted forward to the edge of her chair to get a clear view of all six of us. She started speaking in an even, solemn tone: "It's true that you are none of those things, gentlemen. But I will tell you what you are. You are traitors. And traitors are given the death penalty. If you had enough courage to go out and commit these illegal acts, you ought to have the courage to do what's right. You're hurting America! The substance of these multiple charges are like shots that have been fired on American soil. The men and women of this country didn't fight for it in World War I, World War II, Korea, and Vietnam for you to bring this war here and mess it up with drugs!"

Those who had assisted the government in its investigation, though, she believed were true patriots and she told them so.

"You got on the right side now, so you stay on the right side," she said. "And you tell your family you're on the right side. And tell all those people on the wrong side you're on the American team."

God, she was pissed. I looked back again at the row of lawyers seated behind us, and they were all now swiping their fingers back and forth across their throats to get Teddy to shut the fuck up. But at that time I figured, if the judge was going to bury us under the prison with all that time and money, somebody should just say what we were all thinking. Teddy was so busy getting all that off his chest—and mine, for that matter—that he forgot why he was there. He finally stopped spouting off, except to say:

"Oh . . . um . . . by the way, Your Honor, I plead not guilty!"

On the afternoon of Wednesday, October 19, 1988, the Operation Peacemaker arrests were plastered across the front page of the *Naples Daily News*. The headline read, "Area Part of U.S. Pot Dragnet." The article said that thirty-eight people helped import more than 150 tons, then listed five of those names; the second name on the list was mine, and my holding cell partner Carlos, from earlier, made the first spot. Thirty-nine more were still being sought. The article concluded by reporting that the marijuana had an estimated street value of $147 million. Hot damn! I wish I had known where the fuck that street was located. But the tally of weed wasn't even close. That number represented only what they knew about.

On May 19, 1989, twenty-seven more dudes went down on charges of bringing more than 100,000 pounds of cocaine into the county between 1986 and 1987. On October 11, 1989, forty-eight more were indicted and charged with bringing more than 150,000 pounds of marijuana and more than 3,000 kilograms of cocaine into the country between 1986 and 1988. The arrests marked the end of an era. The freewheeling days of the 1970s and '80s were over. So were the Saltwater Cowboys.

CHAPTER TWENTY-THREE

History is replete with turning points, and this is one such turning point. The end of the Saltwater Cowboys' reign marked an end to Colombian and Jamaican weed coming into the United States. And without a single shot being fired, I might add. This void in the marijuana market also marked a period in history that witnessed America's reintroduction to Mexican brick weed and the ravages of death, destruction, and lawlessness it has brought to our friends south of the border. The plain and simple fact of the matter is that if you were smoking weed in the '70s or '80s, there's a very good chance that we had our hands on it first, proving once again that history is reassuringly filled with written accounts of small groups of people being responsible for satisfying the demand of a larger one. More than two hundred of us went to prison, and those who didn't were the first rats to jump from the burning ship. I hold no animosity toward any of them for the choices they made. There were just too many of us to try to hang on. When you take a bunch of scared kids and threaten them with forty years in prison, they start singing names and they will even toss their grandma in there, too, if they think it will help their case.

As our asses were getting kicked, the United States instituted Operation Just Cause: war in Panama. Our military forces captured General Manuel Noriega, then extradited him to the United States, which ended any safe harboring of our shipments coming from Colombia.

When the indictments were handed down against me and my guys, they consisted of four counts—importation, conspiracy to import, conspiracy with intent to distribute, and possession with intent to distribute more than one thousand kilograms of marijuana—and on top of that a $1 million fine for each count.

Each of these counts also came with a mandatory sentence of ten years to life. Put simply, if we went to trial and were found guilty, we faced a minimum mandatory sentence of forty years to life in prison.

You can't imagine what it's like when someone hands you a piece of paper that reads, "The United States of America versus Tim McBride."

I mean, Jesus.

The most powerful nation on earth was against me. Man, I was screwed! Operation Peacemaker, my ass! There was nothing peaceful about it.

In those days, prison sentences ranged from eighteen months to forty years, so the likely prospect of facing a long prison sentence was enough of an incentive to force a lot of the guys to cooperate with the authorities. By doing so, guys would receive sentences below the mandatory minimums in accordance with US law. Under those new sentencing guidelines, if guys cooperated, they were found guilty on only one count of their indictment. They were also given immunity for all of their other criminal activities, with no fines levied against them. The guidelines opened a large window of freedom for those who had not yet been arrested. Guys who were free on bond told the other dudes, hey, when they arrest you, and they will, take their offer to cooperate. You can give them our names because we have immunity. Everybody took the deal and ratted on one another without hurting themselves or their friends in order to receive a lesser sentence. It was brilliant. But when it came to me, there weren't any names above me that I could give to them. I was categorized as managerial level. The Feds were no longer interested in small fish. They wanted the big boys who I was working with in Miami and Colombia.

I was taken from my county jail cell and placed in leg and belly chains. I was escorted outside and down to the federal building. Whisked off the street through a side door, I was led down a dimly lit hallway that had a musty odor of old books and taken into a small room with one folding metal chair and a big glass window that divided the room into two. On my side of the glass was a microphone and speaker. On the other side of the glass stood a man and a woman dressed in identical brown vested suits.

I sat down on that cold folding chair and they placed against the glass their little gold badges that read "US Treasury Department."

"Oh shit, here we go again," I said out loud.

An assistant US attorney came into the room and joined the two brown-clad Feds. She was the prosecutor. She heard me curse at the sight of the badges.

"No! No! Relax!" she said. "This is not what you think it is."

"Well then, Miss Susan," I asked politely, "why don't you tell me what this is about?"

"Mr. McBride, because of your reluctance to cooperate with regards to your Cuban and Colombian partners—"

I cut her off right there in midsentence.

"Yeah, that's right," I said. "Just shoot me now and shoot my family—"

Then she cut me off.

"Stop. I understand. What it is we would like to know, and that is if you are willing to tell us, please explain how you and the others were able to import these huge amounts of drugs for so many years without our knowledge?"

Was she kidding me? After chasing me around the backwaters, woods, and scrub brush of Florida, all she wanted to know was how we did it?

Hell, the game was over. I could tell her all about that—but without names.

"Please don't take this the wrong way," I told her with a smile on my face, "but your people aren't very smart about this sort of thing. In fact, they're totally clueless. Most of the time the stuff went, quite literally, right past your people."

Then I began to tell these two treasury agents about payoffs to people in almost every branch of law enforcement. Still no names. They could figure those out for themselves. They also learned that when this area became too hot, our loaded boats could dock or sit at anchor in Panamanian or Mexican waters and remain there unmolested until our coast was clear.

"Have you ever seized a vessel loaded with pot or cocaine that was also carrying a large sum of cash?" I asked her.

"Yes," she said.

"Why do you think that cash was there?"

She didn't know.

"It was there because it wasn't used. If our coast was clear, then it wasn't necessary to pay anyone in Panama or Mexico to safeguard the load."

I spent a couple of hours telling them how it was done because, what the hell, it didn't really matter anymore. The game was over.

She stood up to leave, and I asked her one more question:

"Why is all of this so important to you now?"

"Because we just want it to stop and make sure it's stopped," she said.

"Well, you stopped it, didn't you?"

"Yes," she said. "We did."

While in jail, I read stories in the newspaper of a suspicious plane crash that resulted in the death of a guy we all knew very well. He was one of us. I saw on the news that a pipe bomb exploded in a pickup truck, killing the father of another one of the guys, who had been the target. Based on my decade of experience working and hauling for clients whose business ethics I had no control over, it seemed to me that someone out there was taking these guys out. Neither of the two guys who got killed had been indicted. That was because they were two of the original gang who had kicked over the first domino by ratting us out. A few other rats were placed in protective custody after the bombs started going off. I realized then how the government had taken us down. They had gotten hold of a few guys inside our group, threatened them with a shitload of time, and turned them against us. From this simple course of action I've concluded that when it comes to trust, we're depending on our feelings and instincts to guide us, and sometimes they inadvertently let us down.

I was visited four times by investigators during the seven and a half months I was locked down in that county jail. On one occasion, they administered a polygraph. Apparently, they were reluctant to accept that what I was telling them was the truth. But the sobering results of their test proved to them that for years they had seriously underestimated our tenacity. They reacted to the results of my polygraph with the bewilderment of a child who has flunked a test he thought he would certainly ace. I could only tease them.

"You guys nearly caught us several times over the years," I said. "But you didn't. Hell . . . you guys even shot at our boats on more than one occasion. But you missed!"

My high-priced attorney from Baltimore negotiated a plea agreement to avoid going to trial. In that agreement, the government stated that it would drop all counts in the indictments—except one. If I agreed to the plea, the government would sentence me to no more than twenty years without parole. I agreed because, thanks to all of the guys who told prosecutors that I was The Man, the evidence against me was compelling. My crew's testimony against me was stacked four inches high on my attorney's desk.

I had heard that some guys took a chance at trial and ended up with sentences of thirty to sixty years in prison. Screw that! I knew what I faced. Like I said, the freewheeling days were over.

When sentencing day arrived, the cops walked me into the courtroom and sat me down next to my attorney. My dad, brother Pat, and a couple of friends had come down for the sentencing. I raised my handcuffed wrists as a wave to them. I really appreciated the fact that they had come. I expected the worst from the court. This was the same judge who had told me that I not only had disgraced America but also had offended the sacrifice of old soldiers who had died forty years before I was born. She was an old bat, all right, with blue veins sticking out of her neck and forehead that looked like they would explode, causing a stroke that she, unfortunately, did not have. Sunlight beamed through the window behind her and highlighted her graying hair and cast her shadow all the way across the courtroom to where I was sitting. She had a scowl on her face and wore those damn reading glasses with a chain attached.

"I hope that by now, Mr. McBride, you realize the seriousness of these proceedings," she said without a hint of emotion. "You are considered by this court to have been the organizer of the crimes for which so many men have come before me."

She said that she appreciated my considerable insight into our world. She thanked me for not wasting her time on a lengthy trial that, she believed, would have surely had a more disagreeable outcome for me.

"You're welcome, Your Honor," I said. "I apologize to the court."

Better late than never to kiss her ass.

Now came the moment that would determine my fate and define the rest of my life. My dad, brother, and friends slid to the edges of their seats and listened as she sentenced me.

Ten years. Without parole.

After pronouncing the sentence, she felt that she needed to add justification.

"The amount of time I have given you is the direct result of a recommendation that was handed down to me by the United States Attorney's Office."

She had sentenced me under the old guidelines, which would have allowed for parole. But she found a statute under those old laws that didn't. The old battle-ax was having the last laugh.

"Mr. McBride, if I ever see you again or hear that you're in this court being charged with anything to do with what you are here for today, I will see to it that you are warehoused for the rest of your life."

She asked if she would ever see me in her court again.

"No, Your Honor, you won't."

My family and friends cried like babies, but I was somewhat relieved and sad, in my own way. I was relieved that she hadn't given me twenty years, considering how pissed off she had been eight months earlier. And I was sad because I made my father cry.

CHAPTER TWENTY-FOUR

Rolly listened to my verbal diarrhea as the story spilled out. The story of how I explained to the investigators how the Saltwater Cowboys had smuggled pot under law enforcement's noses for years. Without naming names, I had told them how we paid certain individuals to look the other way and how we cooled our jets in foreign waters until the coast was clear. I explained how we transported marijuana from ship to shore to safe house, every step of the process. I answered their questions and cooperated.

I didn't tell them everything they wanted to know. I never named my friends in South America or Miami. But I had cooperated with their questioning about how we had smuggled so much pot into the United States.

From a legal standpoint, that cooperation was going to make all the difference for me.

Rolly listened to every last word. He sat up, kicked his chair over, and said to me, "I think you know what you have to do."

For the next three weeks, I worked on nothing but my own case. I had the tools I needed to petition the court for a reduced sentence, and I finished my brief. A friend on the outside knew an attorney who was willing to present my plea to the same court and the same judge who sentenced me. The clerk set a date for my case to be heard, and Her Honor would rule on it at that time.

The day I received the notice of that hearing, I waited in line for hours to make a phone call home to ask my brother Pat if he would attend and let me know the judge's decision. Pat said he would go to the hearing and report back what the judge decided. But I would have to call him that day. He couldn't call me to let me know.

The years behind bars had trained me in the prisoner's art of doing time. But that training failed me during the seven days before those proceedings. For years I hadn't looked at a calendar. For years I had been unaware of the date unless I asked someone for the purpose of applying it to a document. I just didn't care. There was no reason for me to know, and now was no time to start.

But after a few restless nights I blew it and started a mental countdown, if for no other reason than to ease my anxiety. I couldn't help myself. This hearing would define my life for the next seven years. So, on the night of that seventh day, I waited those few hours in line to hear my brother's voice on the phone. I was so anxious about calling him, I dialed a wrong number twice. On the next try I took a deep breath and slowly dialed it again.

The third time was the charm. I tried to look all calm as I tapped my fingers nervously on the wall. Pat answered, and the operator told him that he was receiving a collect call from an inmate at a federal correctional institution. Did he want to accept the charges?

Silence. I stopped breathing.

"Yes, I'll accept," Pat said. "Hello—"

I cut him off.

"What happened? What did I get?"

"Man," he said, "were you screwin' that prosecutor chick or what? Because she spoke very highly of you."

I could hardly breathe.

"No, goddamn it! Cut the shit and tell me what the old bat said!"

"She cut your sentence to four years."

I was not in the mood to be messed with.

"C'mon, man! Don't fuck with my head!"

At most, I had hoped she might shave off a year or two. But four years?

"I'm not shittin' you, man. She cut you to four years!"

I started yelling and screaming, with a line of cons behind me, waiting to use the phone.

"No way, man! No fuckin' way!"

I screamed. I laughed. I fell over and almost pulled the phone out of the wall. My argument had won the day in a court of law.

I couldn't believe that I was now three months short. Three months from getting out and going home. I would be free! Free from that living hell.

The next morning at breakfast I broke the good news to Rolly. He was so damn excited, and I was, too. But then I was doused with profound sadness. The tears welled when I realized that I would be going home, but he would be staying. At the same time I realized that I would not be able to fulfill the promise I had made to George when he walked out. It was the last thing I had said to him before he left. It was the promise that I would come to see him and we could finally shake hands and embrace each other as free men.

When there are fewer days ahead than there are behind in prison, one begins to awaken for the prison dream. And as it got closer to the day I would be released from that place, I found myself once again beginning to struggle against the emotional ebbs and flows created by an ocean of those dreams. The men whose backs I had watched for years and who had watched mine were being left behind.

Rolly and a few other friends threw me a convict's going-away party the night before my release. Each of them had pitched in a little bit of their commissary snacks and a few other goodies that were bought from a con who worked in the kitchen. There were sodas and ham-and-cheese sandwiches along with an assortment of crackers, chips, and Little Debbie cakes. The dip was made with the noodles from an instant-soup package. Miracle Whip, onions, and peppers stolen from the kitchen completed the recipe. It doesn't sound like much, but to us it was a feast. The tradition for anyone who was leaving was to give away everything he had of value to his friends. Just like my pal Richie had done on the eve of his leaving except for one big difference: my ride home would be paid for by the Bureau of Prisons.

My last day was what the prison called your "walk around" day. I was given a free pass, which meant I could go anywhere within the prison and not be subject to controlled movement. I recall the illusion for what it was: a cold, hollow sense of freedom. I was also not expected to work that day. However, I was expected to get the signature of each of the day's supervising officers on that pass.

At three thirty that afternoon, during lockdown and before four o'clock count, I was escorted to the front office. I changed from my prison clothes into civilian clothes that looked like they were supplied by the local Goodwill. But who gives a shit? I wasn't going to a fashion show. I was going home. All of the items that I chose to take home with me were searched through by the guards, put in a box, and taped shut. The warden showed up to give me his ceremonial going-home speech. He shook my hand and wished me good luck, then handed me an envelope containing a bus ticket and the balance from my account, plus the traditional $125 in cash. I squinted my eyes from the sun reflecting on the shiny linoleum floor as we walked down that long hallway toward the front doors. I pushed my way through them, skipped down the steps, and climbed into a Bureau of Prisons van that was waiting to take me to the bus station. On the way there, the guard who was driving actually spoke to me as if I were just some guy he had picked up hitchhiking.

"Where are you headed?"

That caught me totally by surprise. One minute I'm a piece-of-shit convict being led around by my nose, and the next minute I'm Mr. Joe Blow, the average everyday citizen. I suppressed my resentment toward the guard for being an ignorant hack and feigned interest in his half-assed attempt at conversation.

"I'm headed home to Naples," I mumbled.

I really didn't want to talk to that asshole. I just wanted to get on that bus because all I was hearing now was . . . blah-blah-blah, and he was giving me a fucking headache! The ass wipe got me to the bus station, and like the true piece of shit that I knew he was, he gave me one last dig of the spur.

"Keep your nose clean, and stay out of trouble, ya hear me, boy?"

It was all I could do to keep my cool.

"Kiss my ass, you fuckin' dickhead!"

I strode through those bus terminal doors with a big smile on my face and walked over to a bench and sat down. My bus left in forty minutes.

I cradled a few sacred items under my arm and boarded the bus with about a dozen others behind me. I have to say that I felt really out of place on that bus. It had been four years since I had been in any kind of vehicle at all, let alone two in one day, and one of those was full of ordinary everyday people. The last bus ride I had taken was with thirty or so convicts, and we were all chained to the floor.

This time, some young punk sat a couple seats away, and after about twenty miles down the road, he started up a conversation. He went on about his everyday bullshit problems, where he was going and why . . . yak-yak-yak. I really wanted to bitch-slap that little shit but held it back.

"Look, pal," I said, cutting him off, "I just got out of prison, and if you'll excuse me, I have no idea what the fuck you're talkin' about, and frankly . . . I don't give a shit."

He cranked his head around hard and fast and said, "No shit! How long were you in?"

"Four years. Now shut the fuck up!" Thinking that was the end of it, I settled in and got comfortable.

For a half hour, that little punk chirped one question after another until my convict instincts took over. I stood up, leaned over his seat, and in a voice loud enough for the old lady in the shitter to hear, I said, "One more word out of you, you little prick, and I'll knock you the fuck out and wake you when your stop comes up!"

He immediately rose from his seat and moved to a new one a few rows back. I could have found a more polite way to end our dialogue, but I hadn't yet begun to make that transformation.

Thirty minutes later the punk's stop was up and he dashed off. Only four of us were left on the bus, including me. Two older ladies sat in the back next to the shitter. A couple of rows ahead of them a young girl slept with her head resting on a backpack. There were still nearly three hours left of the ride home when the bus driver stole my attention.

"Would you mind changing seats and maybe moving up here just behind me? C'mon up, son. Keep me company for a while."

I ignored him at first. I didn't want to keep a damn bus driver company. I looked at his reflection in that big mirror above his head and finally thought, *What the hell. Why not?*

I sat in my new seat and listened to him talk to me through that big mirror. With each glance, we settled into what would be a most unforgettable conversation.

"How long were you down, son?"

I glanced up at him with a puzzled look on my face.

"Excuse me?"

"I've been drivin' this bus out of that station for over ten years now," he said, "and I've seen a hundred guys just like you, and I've talked with most of them."

This guy had my attention now.

"How the hell did you know I was in prison?"

"Just by the way you talk, son. You say 'yes, sir' and 'no, sir' or 'yes, ma'am' and 'no, ma'am' to everyone that speaks to you. So you're either in the military or you just got out of that federal prison down the road from the bus station. Judging by your long hair and the way you hammered the last guy who just got off, I'm guessing it has nothing to do with the military."

Over the next three hours that driver and I had a down-to-earth conversation that took me out of my state of mind. He led me to a place where, until now, only books had been able to take me. All I could see of him was a face in the mirror and the back of his head. He was obviously of Asian descent. He wore his long shiny black hair in a braided ponytail, and the reflection in the mirror revealed a face with big dark round eyes and Fu Manchu–style facial hair. We greeted each other with an exchange of our names, and as we talked, I slowly began to realize that I had met a man who wore his emotions on his sleeve. He took out his wallet and introduced me to his family. He spoke with compassion; he talked *to* me and not *at* me. He was almost reverent in the way he spoke of his wife and kids. He talked about their jobs and what they did for one another as a family. It seemed important to him to express how much he loved them. He even mentioned what a great cook his wife had become since they were married. There appeared to be no end to his praise. He described the way his wife took care of the house they had in the country just outside of Tallahassee. How she would wait up for him when he had a late-night run, like the one he was on now. He told stories about how he had gotten into trouble a few times as a kid and how his father always came to his rescue, then whipped his ass for it after supper. He even told me about the family dog. It just had puppies, and the little bastards were running all over the house, crapping on everything. Those repetitious, mundane, and everyday events were things he cherished, like those precious little treasures you've keep tucked away in a tattered cardboard box that you've saved since your childhood.

I mostly listened, laughed, and stared at the endless hypnotic flashing of white lines as they zoomed toward me in the headlights. His stories became a warm blanket that wrapped around me, and with each word he spoke, it got a little cozier. I cannot for the life of me remember his name, but every time I think about him, I wish to God I could. For all I knew he could have been an angel sent not only to take me down that road and deliver me home but also to deliver me from the chaos and the fear that had occupied my mind for four years. He had a mystical air about him and a mesmerizing, gentle tone to his voice. As we got closer to my stop, I wished there were a thousand miles to go.

We pulled into the bus station in downtown Fort Myers as the sound of air brakes announced our arrival. The few passengers were gathering their things and preparing to make their way to the exit. The bus driver turned around in his seat and put his hand on my shoulder.

"We have no power over which direction the wind blows; however, we can adjust our sails," he said. "From now on, when you wake up each morning, remind yourself of what it felt like to step down from my bus a free man. At some point during each day, let that certain someone who is closest to your heart know how much you love them. Take nothing for granted because the most precious possessions you'll ever have in your life are the simplest. Always be proud of yourself. You're evolving, my man. It's time to move on."

And last but most important of all, he said, "Offer comfort to a stranger as if he were a friend. Because if one day you should happen to meet someone as I have met you, and you see the confusion and uncertainty in their eyes like that which I see in yours, and you can sense the pain and the anger in their heart like that which I sense in yours, then offer them your hand as I offer you mine and give to them that which I have just given to you."

We clasped right hands and shook as friends do; then with his left hand he reached out to me, pulled me close, and said, "You're not that kid that went into prison. You're the man that walked out. I'm telling you this, my young friend, because ten years ago *I* walked out and left behind fifteen years of my own life in D-unit."

The young girl had left, and two old ladies from the back were the last to leave, so my new friend stepped down from his bus to assist them, and I followed. The clock struck midnight. Nothing more needed to be said between us except good-bye and good luck.

My sister-in-law Becky waited to pick me up. We had about a thirty-minute ride to the small community of Golden Gate, just east of Naples, where my brother Pat had built a home for them and their three kids. When I got into the car, I felt awkward for reasons I could not explain. I had a terrible feeling that I was somewhere that I shouldn't be, and I found it very hard to get comfortable riding in that car. The narcotic effect of that bus driver's voice wore off, and I faced the realities of being home. I wasn't prepared for it. To be honest, up until that moment, I hadn't realized that I needed any preparation. I wasn't ready to deal with the thoughts and feelings I was having. I felt like a visitor from another world. I stared out the window quietly as tears began to cloud my eyes.

Can this be what George was feeling even before he left prison? I asked myself.

I could see him trying to tear out of his skin and shed himself of this terrible dread of returning to civilization. Dennis's voice from eight months before echoed:

"One day, God forbid, you and I might experience the same thing."

I had been there only for four years, but he was there for thirty-one. My God, how did he ever bring himself to walk out of there? I never had anticipated the effects this sudden reintegration would have on me.

Then I remembered how I had helped him gain the courage to suck it up and walk through those doors and into another life. I wiped my eyes with my sleeve and whispered to myself.

"It's your turn to suck it up, Tim."

We arrived at the house, and I stood outside the car for a moment, taking in the silence of the evening and contemplating my future. I raised my hand to the night sky and held the full moon between two fingers. Men my age had left their footprints on its surface, and I knew, having endured everything I had, that all things were possible.

It was very late. My brother, niece, and twin nephews were sound asleep. I went to my room, set my duffel bag and my box full of everything I owned on the floor. I stripped down to my underwear like I had done for so many years, and I climbed into bed. The absence of noise in the house was disturbing, to say the least. I had become accustomed to falling asleep each night listening to a lullaby of voices, grunts, and snoring accompanied by the occasional rattling of keys and the banging of a steel door. I closed my eyes and imagined myself already asleep and that this was just a dream. Eventually the stress and exhaustion of the day's events caught up with me. I fell asleep, only to awake sitting straight up, not remembering that I was home. Just as I realized where I was, my brother and his three kids burst through the door and jumped on me, giggling and shouting.

"Welcome home, Uncle Tim!"

Tears welled up in his eyes as Pat wrapped me in a big bear hug and whispered right into my ear.

"It's great to have you home, little brother," he said, voice cracking. "I've missed you."

Work couldn't wait, so Pat took off. My first day home was spent getting to know my niece and my twin nephews. Wrestling around the house all day and throwing pillows at these little kids was a wonderful diversion from the thoughts that were tearing me apart. But there were terrifying moments throughout the day when I would suddenly stop whatever I was doing and, in a panic, wonder if I was out of bounds. Several times I stopped and wondered if I had forgotten to call my parole officer.

When I had been sentenced four years earlier, I hadn't been eligible for parole. Now they had given me three years of supervised release. In my opinion, there was really no difference. I still had to report to a piece-of-shit parole officer once a month. If I failed to report to him for any reason, or if I failed in any way to abide by his rules, he could send me back. I would then have to start from scratch and do the entire three years all over again in prison. The BOP still had their claws in me, and this dickhead would send me back even if I was on my last day of supervision. So on top of being fucked up in the head from dealing with my release, I had the added pressure of dealing with that prick, too.

One of the terms of my supervision stated that I must have a job within one week of my release. Fortunately, prior to my coming home, Pat had arranged for me to work for him. So I used that week to try to get my shit together. During that time, each afternoon when Pat got home, we would have dinner, then just sit in the living room and talk. A few nights had passed, and while relaxing and bullshitting, he sat up and grabbed a deck of cards from under the coffee table. He shuffled them, and he asked me if I wanted to play a few hands. Pat and I had always enjoyed playing cards. We had fond memories of growing up playing all sorts of card games with my grandmother. I hesitated for a moment, closed my eyes, and told him, "No, thanks. I don't think so."

I explained to him that after my last game with George, I had not picked up a deck of cards and I probably would not again.

"George?" he asked. "Who's George?"

EPILOGUE

I remember those first weeks in prison as if they were yesterday. When the bus rolled up to the gates on that cold November evening in 1989, I got my first glimpse of the prison yard. I also got my first glimpse of those stone-cold, red brick and steel-barred buildings that were never warm. They were like something you'd see in a late-night horror movie. It was raining sideways, and the sky was overcast. The prison itself was backlit by purple storm clouds looming in the distance that spewed jagged shards of lightning. Out of the darkness the flashes were taking snapshots of a dozen rain-soaked convicts, freezing them in time as they did the prisoner shuffle into the first of those red brick buildings. It's called the prisoner shuffle because that's the only way you can walk when both of your ankles are shackled and chained together.

When we got inside the building, we were herded into a steel-caged holding cell, where our handcuffs, belly chains, and leg shackles were removed. Then we were told to strip, and the guards searched us from head to toe. One by one they took us from that cage to be examined by a prison doctor. When Dr. Knuckles was finished spelunking around in our asses, we were sent down the line to be issued new clothes. True to their pissant generosity, they bestowed upon each of us a pair of underwear, a new orange prison jumpsuit, and a used pair of dark-blue slip-on canvas deck shoes. From there we formed another line to receive a bedroll that consisted of a piece-of-shit pillow wrapped in a sheet and a scratchy wool blanket. After all that bullshit they took us single file up two flights of stairs, through a set of locked steel doors into E-unit. E-unit was the admissions and orientation section of the prison. There we were given our bunk assignments, and there we stayed until the prison staff tested us to determine our level of education—but also, more important, to determine if the crime we were there for would put us at risk when placed in general population. For instance, if you were convicted of rape, child molestation, or any type of crime that involved sexual battery of any kind, you were as good as dead if they put you in with the general population. When they were satisfied that you weren't at risk, it was just a matter of waiting until a bunk space opened up in one of the regular housing units. They made us wear those fucked-up orange jumpsuits until we were moved out, like a bull's-eye drawn on our backs—everyone knew we were the new fish.

I'll never forget my first walk to the chow hall. Our unit had just been let out to go eat dinner. Walking outside for the first time in months without chains, I was taking it all in. It was a pretty depressing sight. The chow hall was on the opposite end of the inner compound. On the right was A-unit and B-unit. They were built end to end, separated in the middle by a laundry room. In it were five washers and five dryers that were available for use by any prisoner who chose to do his own laundry. On the left, C-unit and D-unit were set up the same way. A network of sidewalks coming from all six buildings crisscrossed through finely manicured grass and connected to a circle in the middle, where the flagpole stood.

My third step into the new realm was on the grass. I had cut across an area where the sidewalks met at an angle, and I kept going. A few steps later I heard a voice behind me screaming. "Hey, you . . . Inmate, stop right there!"

I didn't turn around to look because whatever was going on was certainly none of my business. No sooner had I gotten that thought out of my head than a guard came up from behind, jumped out in front of me, and in a voice characteristic of a drill sergeant asked me, "Did you just step on my grass back there, boy?"

I was dumbfounded.

"Yeah, I think I did."

"Well! I don't *think* you did! I *know* you did!" he screamed sarcastically. "I'll tell you what you're gonna do now, boy. When you're done havin' chow, you're gonna come back out here and find me!"

"Yes, boss," I told him.

I went and had my dinner. When I got back outside, I walked up to the son of a bitch like he had told me.

"C'mon with me," he said.

We walked over to the spot of grass that I stepped on, and he pointed to it, saying, "You need to get down on your hands and knees and apologize to my grass."

I looked at him and thought that guy was nuttier than a piece of rat shit in a pecan factory.

"While you're down there, I want you to go over this entire area with a fine-toothed comb and pick up everything that isn't grass. I want matches, I want cigarette butts, I want paper, and I'll then tell you when you're done."

He reached into his pocket and pulled out a small clear plastic bag and handed it to me. For two hours I picked up crap out of that asshole's grass; then he came back and snatched the bag from my hand and said, "From now on stay off my grass, boy! Now get outta my face!"

My first week was taken up with classes that were held in the education building. The first class was administered by the warden. He felt that it was his responsibility to personally instruct new fish in the rules and regulations of the prison. The warden also felt that it was his responsibility to let each of us know that if we did not have a high school diploma, we would most certainly be getting one. We took tests to ascertain our level of education. If your test score reached the equivalent of or exceeded a twelfth-grade level, you could move on into general population and be assigned to a regular housing unit. If you scored below that level, you would remain in the admissions and orientations building until you achieved that level. It was determined that my education level was that of a third-year college student. Thank God, now it was only a matter of time before I was removed from that cattle pen where I was living.

I spent three more weeks in that shithole before finally being assigned to a unit with an open bunk space. When my name was called and my assignment handed to me, I was instructed to head down to the laundry, where I would be issued new prison uniforms, a bedroll, and a pillow. I was given three of everything: three shirts, three pairs of pants and shorts, three pairs of socks, three pairs of underwear and T-shirts. With my new wardrobe in hand and bedroll and pillow under my arm, I walked into A-unit and was given my bunk assignment by the unit guard. After eleven months of being locked down in steel cages, I was finally walking into the place I would call home for the next nine years and one month.

The first thing I did was make up my bunk. It was on top. The bottom bunks had to be earned over time. They were down low and relatively out of sight and were coveted. Guys have to wait until someone is either paroled or dies before they can make a move.

The second thing I did was take off that damned orange jumpsuit and put on a pair of pants and a shirt. I threw that jumpsuit in the collection barrel next to the exit door, then began to take a tour of my new house. It really wasn't that bad considering where I had just been. It was a dormitory-style setup. The linoleum floor was polished to a mirror finish; the block walls also shimmered with dozens of layers of glossy enamel paint. The ceiling was vaulted, and the hundred-by-fifty-foot room was lined with four rows of steel-walled cubicles. Each cube had all the comforts of home, a set of bunk beds, two lockers, a desk, and two folding chairs. At that end of the building was the TV room, and next to it was a locked wooden door with blinds covering the window laminated with wire mesh. That was the room where I would meet every six months with a team of counselors, prison administrators, and guards who would be evaluating my custody level along the way. I ambled to the other end of the building, where the toilets and showers were located. Those facilities weren't much to look at, but at least they were clean. For the next forty-five minutes, controlled movement had me restricted to the unit, so I took this time to acclimate to my new surroundings. After a leisurely stroll around my new home, I took the folding chair that was next to my locker and went into the TV room. It had been months since I'd watched anything. Sure, there had been a TV just about everywhere I went before landing here, but you couldn't hear it above all the commotion. Trying to watch it was a waste of time. But now I was the only one in the room. All the other guys were either working or out in the yard. My favorite program was about to start, so I settled in and lost myself in the latest episode of *Star Trek: The Next Generation*. It was a rare treat—not just because I was alone and able to enjoy the show but also because the room was air-conditioned. The rest of the unit wasn't. The solitude and cool comfort of that room provided me with something I hadn't experienced for almost a year: total silence. What the hell, my work assignment with the prison construction crew didn't start until tomorrow, so I stayed in there the entire afternoon until three thirty lockdown.

Four o'clock count kicked off the dinner hour, and controlled movement between the inner compound and rec yard was terminated until nine thirty, when they locked us down for the night.

Exiting the chow hall with a bellyful of hamburgers and French fries, I took my first walk around the rec yard. There was a full-size soccer field on the upper yard surrounded by a running track. To the right of that were the six racquetball courts. Spread out over the lower rec yard were the weight pile, softball field, basketball court, sand-filled volleyball court (nicknamed "peter beach"), and I'll be damned if they didn't have a nine-hole miniature golf course. I hung around the volleyball court for most of the evening and even got in on a few games. It was unlike any volleyball game I had ever played. The cons called it "jungle ball," and they played it using prison rules. They were easy to follow because there were only two of them: the ball was either in bounds, or it was out of bounds. This was the only way the game could be played by a bunch of criminals. If there were any more rules, the game would quickly escalate into an all-out brawl.

Nine thirty lockdown and ten o'clock count were close at hand, so I made my way back to the unit. Lying on my bunk, sweating my ass off, I decided there and then that it was time to get myself back into shape. The next day, the weight pile would be my daily hangout, and perhaps I would recruit a workout partner. Being that it was so close to count time and the showers were all occupied, I decided to clean up afterward. The guards came in right on schedule and did their last count for the day. I put on my flip-flops, wrapped a towel around my waist, grabbed my soap and shampoo, then headed for the showers. Minding my own business and walking between the rows of bunks, I tried not to look in on them, but when I passed the last cubicle in the row, I heard a voice call out to me.

"Excuse me, son!"

I was surprised to be addressed in such a polite manner. I stopped dead in my tracks, turned, and looked in. All I could see of the single occupant were his legs sticking out from the bottom bunk. The rest of him was sitting back against the wall of the cubicle, and the shade from the bunk above his head hid his face from my view.

"Hello there," I said. "My name's Tim."

And from the shadow he spoke to me with a slow, melodic Southern drawl.

"Hello there, Timmy. My name's George. You don't happen to know how to play gin rummy, do ya?"

AFTERWORD

I was arrested in October of 1988 and released back into the world on March 3, 1992, to three more years of "special parole." Shortly after, I took on a new adventure and became a father, something I thought I'd never have a chance to experience. As of this writing, my son has just turned twenty-one, and my beautiful daughter is now eighteen. My long nights of running offshore have been traded for even longer days running a construction crew. Déjà vu washed over me as I recalled my first few days home from prison. My brother Pat had a job waiting for me. He was the company's only superintendent at that time, and in just a few months I went from jumping out of the back of his pickup truck with a shovel in my hand, just like the other laborers, to running the entire labor force. I was so fucking glad to have my life back and so fucking glad to be home, I was exploding with energy. Within a year I was the company's new commercial superintendent, running a growing crew of fifty men over the next eleven years. Over the next seven years I assisted in the logistical operations of three more local companies with which I had once competed. Sound familiar? In 2008, when the housing bubble burst, so did my little bubble. I had, by that time, been a divorced single father for five years, and since the divorce, my kids came home with me and did not leave my sight. I found myself sitting at home without a clue as to how I was going to keep a roof over my little family's head and food on the table. Then a thought occurred to me. Before I went to prison, I had more friends than I could count, and when I got home, I could count them all on one hand with a few fingers left over. But through the years, those few friends and I would get together with their friends, and inevitably someone would say, "Hey, Timmy, would you mind telling these guys one of your crazy-ass stories?" And their reactions were always voiced the same: "DAMN! That would make a great book! That shit is fucking nuts!"

On June 25, 2011, I staged a reunion of Saltwater Cowboys at a pub in Naples, Florida. The local press quickly picked up on the story, and the turnout was surprising. I received e-mails and phone calls from pot haulers I never knew. The *Fort Myers News-Press* was there at the party, interviewing people for a Sunday story. A reporter who wanted the viewpoint from the opposing side of marijuana smuggling for the newspaper story contacted supervising agent David Waller, who is currently the resident agent for the Florida Department of Law Enforcement in Lakeland, Florida. It turns out that he was my nemesis back in the day: the man behind the wheel of the tan Bronco that fateful night on Pine Island. He was also the agent who was in charge of my case.

A few months before the Saltwater Cowboys reunion, Agent Waller contacted me, and we had a very pleasant chat. I gave him a *Reader's Digest* condensed version of my life since our last encounter, and he told me that he had recently attended a conference at the federal building in Fort Myers with dozens of agents from around the country. The topic of the conference just happened to be Operation Peacemaker, and my name had been tossed around for most of the day. So out of curiosity he looked me up online, then called me and we became reacquainted. This *News-Press* reporter asked Waller if he believed the stories of how I made more than $25 million smuggling weed. Waller was quoted as saying, "That's a good conservative estimate. McBride had direct contact with marijuana wholesalers from other countries. He was good, a very smooth talker." When the reporter told Waller that I was planning a reunion of the Saltwater Cowboys, he burst into laughter. He wasn't surprised.

I'd like to acknowledge all of those crews out there who worked at this game throughout those years. Whether your loads made it to shore or not, my hat's off to you. To say that my crews were the only ones out there crisscrossing the Caribbean and risking their asses to gain a foothold in this revolution would be just plain insulting. I'm simply saying that because of this labyrinth of the Ten Thousand Islands that Mother Nature constructed in our backyard, we were able to be consistent enough in this game to have integrated smuggling into a way of life spanning three generations.

Ironically, I would not be able to tell my story if I had not gone to prison. My bank-robbing friend Dennis Lehman took me under his wing and taught me how to bare my soul to the pages of a yellow legal pad. I don't expect to get cash rich from this attempt at authoring. But what I do expect is to become rich in the knowledge that, through my testimony, I have done my friends and the little town of Everglades City a bit of justice. It's time to pull back that dark veil of infectious ignorance that has caused them to bow their heads in shame for their long-standing relationship with a plant that, in today's world, is quite benign. The town remains pristine and beautiful, and the hearts and souls remain pure in my many friends who still reside among the mangrove islands. They are the caretakers and the guardians of a vast and beautiful wilderness paradise. And if your travels should bring you to southwest Florida, do yourself a favor and hop on an airboat or take a guided fishing trip into the backcountry of the islands, because you just never know. Your captain might be an old outlaw with a story or two to tell.

Only a handful of Saltwater Cowboys are left who have the knowledge of how the jobs were done. Not even the investigators had this knowledge, as proved by their years of failed and frustrated efforts to capture us. This book is meant to erase the fiction and myths and awaken you to a nonfiction world filled with harsh reality.

Earlier, I wrote that I never once feared for my life. Well, I take that back. The one and only thing that ever threatened my life was the US government. Our government is still playing the bully when it comes to marijuana laws. Properly regulated, this new market has the potential to create a stream of revenue that would change the course of this nation and its economy. It also potentially harbors the cure for cancer, our plague of the twenty-first century, yet the federal government blindly continues to justify the ridiculous and expensive task of criminalizing marijuana. Consider that the typical US citizen isn't going to get caught with more than 150 tons in his pocket when you dwell on the following facts. For having been caught with just under 400,000 pounds, I ultimately served four years in a federal prison. So what is the most powerful nation on the planet saying to its own citizens when it can take more than two hundred potential life sentences for flooding North America with marijuana and reduce them to what amounts to a mere slap on the wrist? Why would it continue today with this childish bullying and posturing when there is a simple truth and a simple fix? The truth is that I wound up with the most time for acting as a manager of this operation, and after being threatened with life in prison four times over, I was handed ten years, and that was ultimately reduced to four. This not only illustrates the insane range of time judges dispense with discretion, but it also points to a rather large inconsistency within individual state and federal sentencing guidelines. I don't know about you, but I think this demonstrates our justice system's inability to level the playing field even in matters left to the judges' own discretion. There is a simple fix to all of this, and it lies within the answer to this next question: Why doesn't Big Brother continue to give out a little of that compassion he gave to my crew and me? Here is an example of that compassion.

After my sentence was pronounced, I was told this by the US attorney who prosecuted me: "We just wanted to stop your activities and give everyone a little time as punishment, Tim. When it came to sentencing, we took very much into consideration the background and type of people with which we were dealing. We discovered that beneath all of this lawlessness, there were nonviolent hardworking men and women, most of whom had their own families. Each case was reviewed one by one, and the wives and children of each family that would be left behind were also taken into consideration. Then a *reasonable* sentence was determined."

I know that Big Brother is out there somewhere reading this, and I want you to know that I'm grateful for the compassion that was ultimately bestowed upon me. But my sincere hope is for that same understanding and compassion to be dispensed equally among all your little brothers and sisters; for that you would have the gratitude of a nation.

While presenting you, the reader, with this twenty-two-year snapshot of my life, I felt it was important for you all to understand

and for me to remind you that—although the men whom I worked with in Miami were shooting it out to see who would ultimately dominate the drug trade—we Saltwater Cowboys weren't violent, nor did we ever carry weapons. We were very much the opposite. We were just a bunch of young, barefooted, modern-day outlaws running these southern waters and the Caribbean on a quest for that one thing in life that we all crave: adventure. We possessed a unique ability that our clients needed, and for this ability they were willing to pay, and they paid very well.

It was this relatively harmless good ol' boy mentality that makes us unique. Couple that with an amazing sequence of events, and it ultimately became the deciding factor in why I'm able to sit here in the comfort of my home and tell you these stories.

Twenty-two years have gone by since my release from prison, and it is only now that I feel comfortable passing these stories along to you. I also feel very passionately that America, as well as the world, should know exactly what we did, how we did it, and the extent to which it was done. In those days there was, and still is, an overwhelming demand for our product. So for nearly two decades our little corner of the world supplied that demand, and it just happened to be for the most popular and the most widely used illegal drug on earth. A plant.

In the wake of the recent changes in legislation regarding marijuana legalization, let me just say, it's about time! I am not going to launch into a one-sided debate on this subject—I'm just hanging up my diploma. I also want to say to the very cool people of my generation and the next that if you're finally willing to step up and join this revolution, then you should at least be introduced to a few of its founding fathers.

In these changing times this story is absolutely relevant in that it reflects a true belief in a thing and a true desire to make that thing a reality. Along with changing times and changing attitudes, there must also be changes in perception and presentation. It's time to remove the stigma that has plagued this little plant and give it a respectable introduction to those who have not been introduced. The days of making midnight runs are over, and there's now a spotlight shining down where there was once shadow. It's time to put marijuana, with all of its wonderful flavors, aromas, and experiences, out there on the shelves and let the people make their own decisions. Human nature, more specifically curiosity, dictates that some of you, in states that have boldly spoken up, who once said you wouldn't will now say you will. Because you have freedom to choose. And that blows my mind!

Author's Note

This book is for all the men and women of Everglades City and Chokoloskee whom I am proud to call my friends and my extended family. This is also their legacy and one for which they should not be solely recognized. Southwest Florida's wilderness frontier was tamed and settled by real men and women who dared to show the world that no matter where on this earth you should choose to call home, Mother Nature will teach you how to provide for your family.

The characters I introduced to you within these pages are spoken of with my utmost respect and admiration. My acknowledgment also extends of course to those whom I did not mentioned, yet I'm comfortable with the fact that if you read this you all know who you are.

However, there is one person I would like to name and honor simply because his vision has allowed my mark on this world to silently remain behind for generations to come. Ernest Hamilton was in no way involved with any of the smuggling activities of which I speak. He was an honest, hardworking, unforgettable sweetheart of a man and a legend in his own right. He and his lovely wife lived just a stone's throw from the hill where we stored and repaired our stone crab traps in the off-season. He was the founder of the only stone crab and fish house on Chokoloskee Island, and it bore his name. At times he would appear among the stacked maze of traps to sit with us and chat. He would spin his yarns of the days when he and men like him literally rowed their trap-laden skiffs in and out of these same passes and how, back in the days before Styrofoam, they used sealed blown-glass spheres wrapped in fish netting for buoys. He lovingly teased us about how easy we had it: "What with diesel engines and hydraulic motors and all."

In the summer of 1983, I was volunteered by my captain along with two others to assist a local architect and chief builder in breaking ground on and constructing an observation tower at the edge of town near the causeway to Chokoloskee Island. Ernest's vision was as tall as a five-story building and was built with heavy rough-cut lumber to ensure that it would withstand the test of time. I was there every day during its construction, from the clearing of the forest in which it stands to the placement of the lightning staff on its peak. To this day I carry within me a sense of personal pride in knowing that all of that hard work was for a simple man whose only wish was to share with travelers the beauty of this place he called home. Sadly this iconic monument has outlasted his historical fish house, which was torn down several years before the writing of this story. Only a bare concrete slab remains where it once stood and serves as the headstone for a bygone era and a treasure lost to the elements and time. Three decades later the tower's timbers are as secure as they were the day we joined them together. And for decades to come Ernest's legacy will stand tall above the mangroves as an example of the fearless and robust determination of the kind of men and women whom he absolutely represents.